SENSE N' STYLE Team

Editor-in-chief - Vine Aduara Oghenekparobo

Marketing Executives
Thais Carvalho
Sierra Morgado
Aaron Price

Staff Writers
Effie Odhiambo
Michelle Njeri Ngarama

Creative Director
Contributing Personas
Valeria Busch
Zen Yezri
Racheal Evans

Magazine's Production Team
Photographers
Richard Berryman
James Nick Merzetti
Alejandro Apodaca
Daniel Chin Photography
Anny Roberts Photography

Make Up Artists
Eva Glez
Leonardo Salinas
Leidy Donovan

CONTACT US

LinkedIn: Sense N' Style Magazine
Instagram: @sense_n_style_magazine
Email: info@sensenstyle.org

www.sensenstyle.com

SENSE N' STYLE

NOV/DEC ISSUE 2024

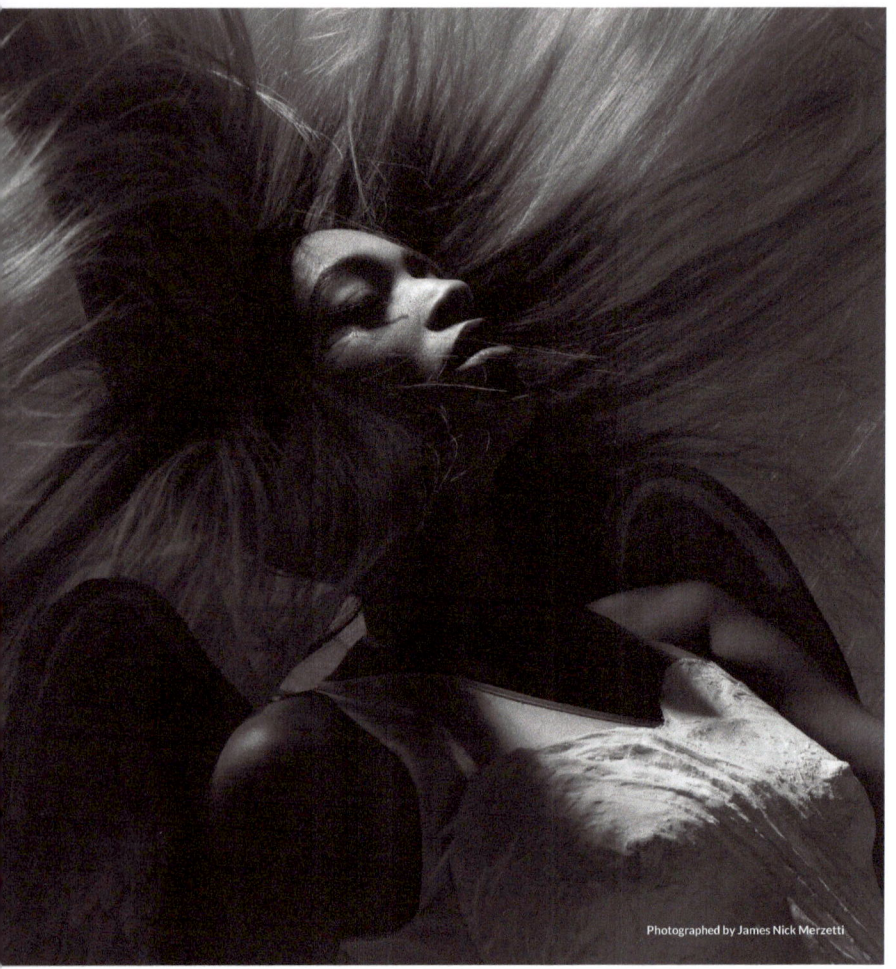

Photographed by James Nick Merzetti

EDITOR'S NOTE — 09
Exploring The Amazing Stories Behind Creatives' Journey: A Brief Overview Of The Theme And Focus Of This Issue

THE HOLIDAY FASHION — 10
Choosing the right outfit for the favorite season of the year!

COCO WALK MIAMI — 12
The Month's Hot Spot Featuring Coco Walk Miami

"Fashion is not just about clothes; it's a reflection of who we are, how we see the world, and how we want the world to see us. It's a language without words, expressing confidence, creativity, and individuality with every choice we make".

EDITORIAL PORTRAITS — pg 14
EXPLORE AN EXCLUSIVE HIGHLIGHT OF ANNY'S ROBERT INTERVIEW WITH SENSE N' STYLE MAGAZINE

THE NEW LUXURY — 16
Discover How Your Dream Car & Your Fashion Sense Intertwines

The Insider Look With Netflix Actress - Michelle Allen — pg 20

INES TROCCHIA — 22
Unveiling the Face Behind the Cover: Ines Trocchia's Bold Journey in Pursuit of Her Dreams

The Guide to Self Love — 28
Our Editor's Special: Deep Dive Into The Perfect Guide to Self Love Through Your Skincare Routine

CULINARY DELIGHTS — 31
A Journey Worth Savoring: Top 5 Restaurants For Traditional Cuisines In Miami

QADIRA — 34
Explore Fashionable Haute Couture Dresses With Qadira Designs

Sense N' Style App - Exclusive Look Into Our Exciting New Project — pg 40

YEAR END MOMENTUM — 42
THE INSIDER'S LOOK: WOMEN EMPOWERMENT

 www.sensenstyle.com
(+1) 857 210 4787 | (591) 70905542
info@sensenstyle.org

SENSE N' STYLE MAGAZINE | 02

SENSE N' STYLE
NOVEMBER/DEC 2024

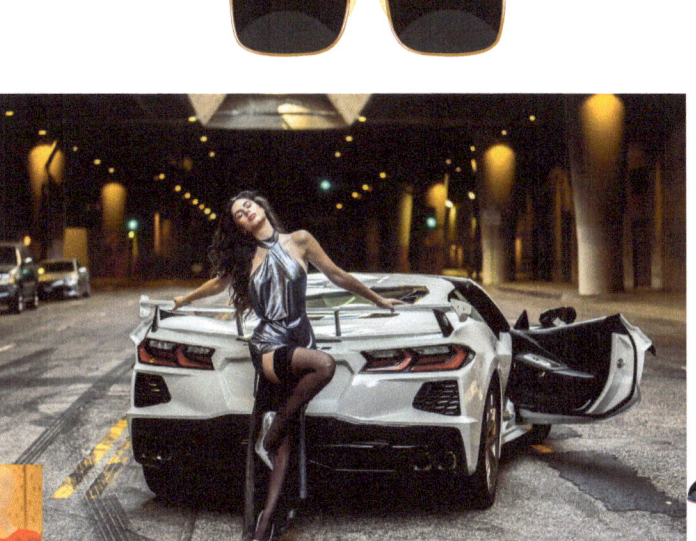

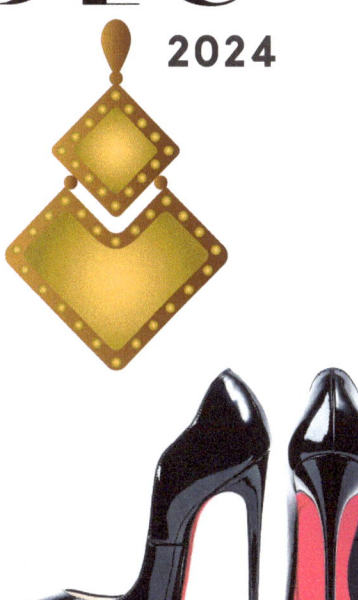

FASHION & LIFESTYLE

MICHELLE ALLEN
An exclusive interview with Michelle Allen as she shares her experience in the fashion and entertainment industry.

INES TROCCHIA
Being passionate about what you do - the key to success! "When your job aligns with your passion, it doesn't feel like work"

QADIRA HAUTE COUTURE
Discover the inspiration driving iconic Bolivian designers Glenda and Rolando as they share a detailed look into their creative journey and the story behind their work.

FEATURED MODELS
1. Michelle Allen
2. Martina Alaiza
3. Lucia Maria
4. Camila Bohrt
5. Kristienne W
6. Iderah_Jawnseen
7. Ebubechukwu Chiejine
8. Bumia Yeri
9. Zuleih
10. Nwanneka Precious
11. Aduke
12. Nicole Kenia

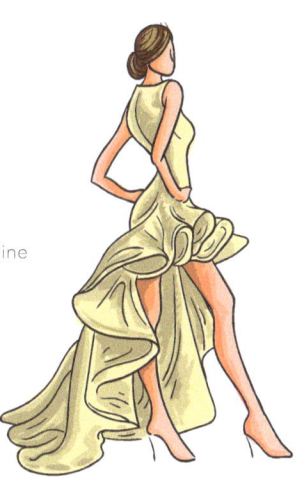

SWITCH IT UP FOR THE BEST TIME OF THE YEAR!
Think classic red or green hues, or even a plaid pattern. You don't need to wear something overly flashy to look stylish.

List of Photographer's Work Featured in this Edition
1. Anny Robert
2. James Nick Merzetti
3. Richard Berryman
4. Alejandro Apodaca
5. Vaughan Treyvellan
6. Justin Muni
7. Kayla MaDonna
8. Daniel Chin
9. Ricardo Photography
10. Micky Angel Vargas

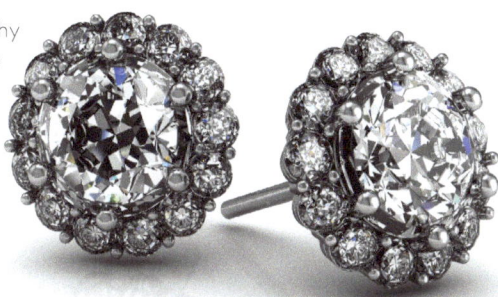

SENSE N' STYLE MAGAZINE | 03

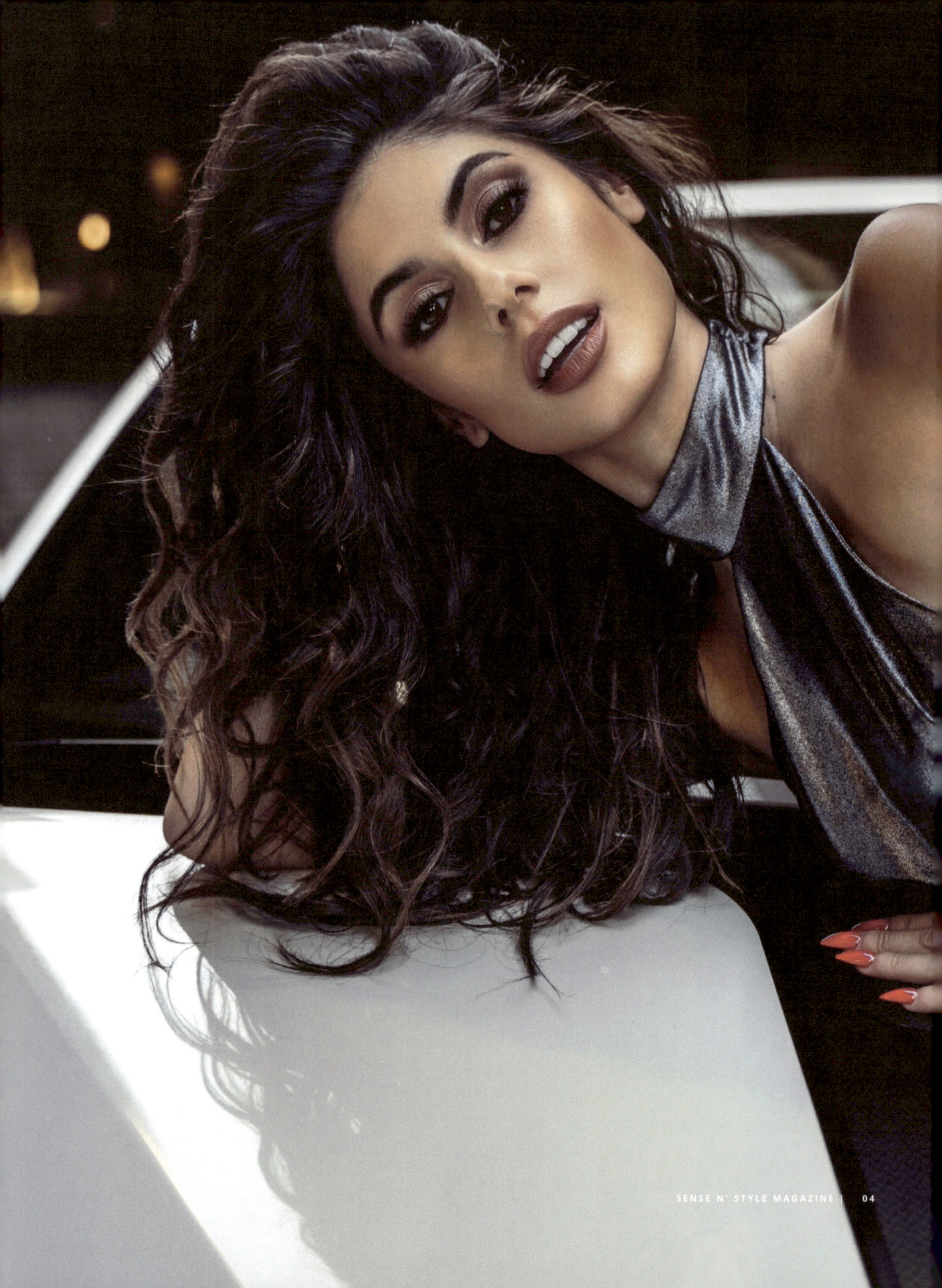

Production Team:

Model: Ines Trocchia
Photographer: Richard Berryman
Styled by: Daniel Alamillo
Make up Artist: Eva Glez

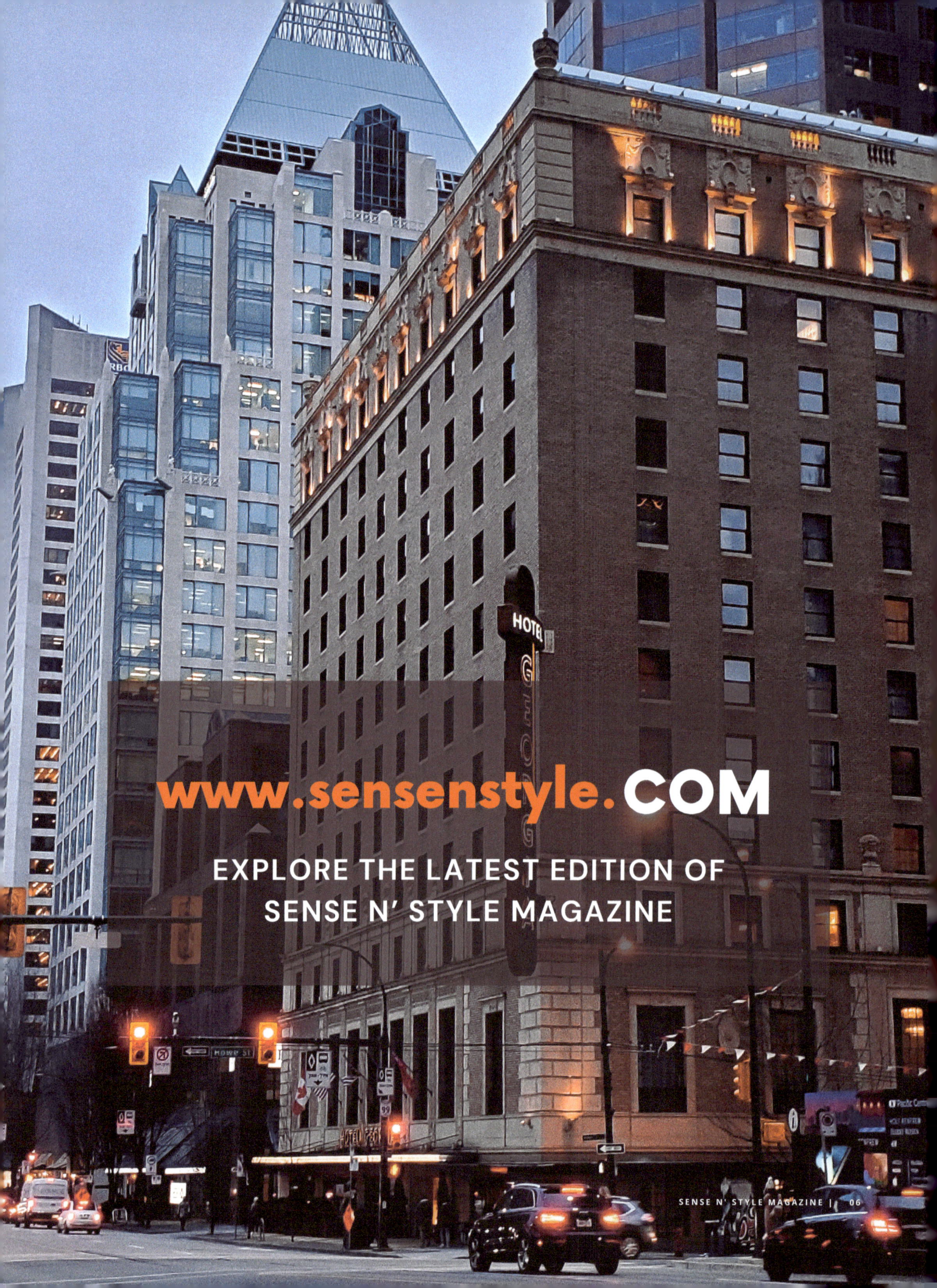

SENSE N' STYLE FASHION

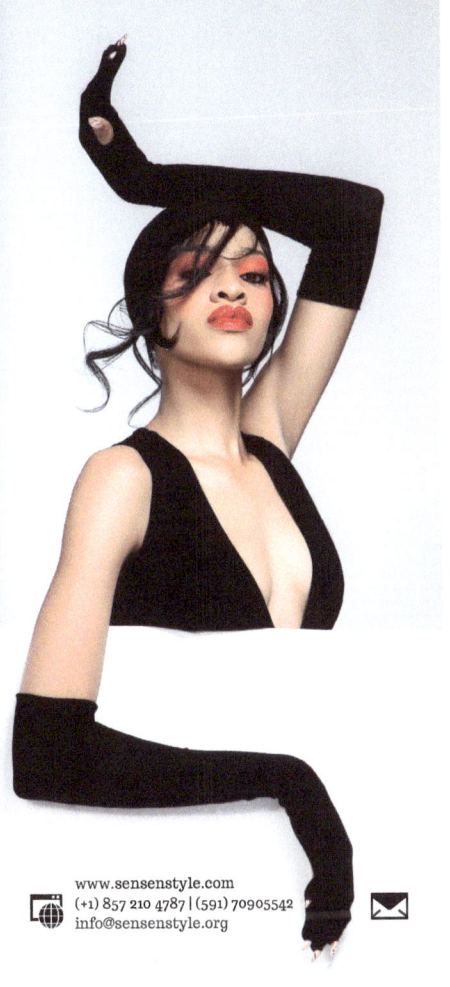

www.sensenstyle.com
(+1) 857 210 4787 | (591) 70905542
info@sensenstyle.org

SPECIAL ARTICLES
Fashion & Lifestyle

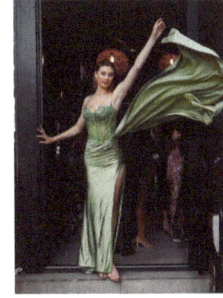

Our fashion articles are available for our audience to keep up with different updates and trends in the fashion industry

Sense N' Style Magazine is a leading provider for news updates and present-day inspiring stories in the fashion & entertainment industry. Our Magazine disseminates fashion news, latest styles, new businesses, and inspiring stories to our readers.

With a team of experts boasting extensive experience in the field, our aim is to provide our readers with all the novelties of fashion easily accessible for them to learn current trends.

SKINCARE: A GUIDE TO SELF LOVE

Applying a face mask or massaging in a moisturizer isn't just about your skin; it's about creating space to slow down, breathe, and give yourself attention

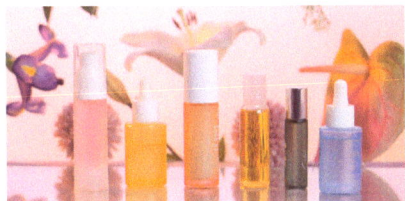

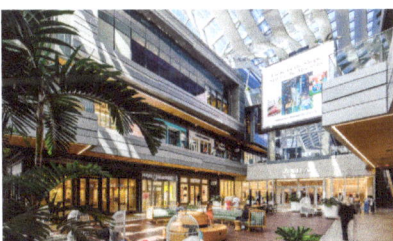

COCO WALK MIAMI

You can grab a bite, sip on coffee, or even catch a movie after you're done exploring the stores. The whole experience feels laid back yet upscale, which is very Miami.

40 SNSM LATEST APP

Get an Inside Look at Sense N' Style's New App, Created to Connect Fashion Professionals Across the Industry

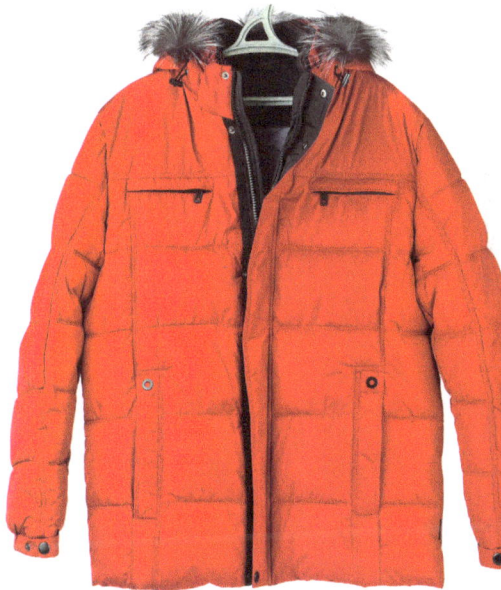

31 CULINARY DELIGHTS

Discovering Top Restaurants In Miami For Traditional Cuisine

Whether you're indulging in classic Cuban flavors, savoring fresh seafood, exploring the fusion of East and West, or immersing yourself in the art scene, Miami's top restaurants offer a feast for the senses.

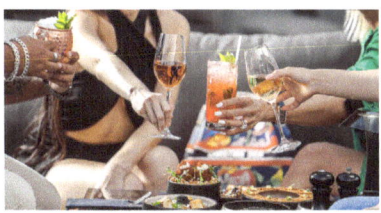

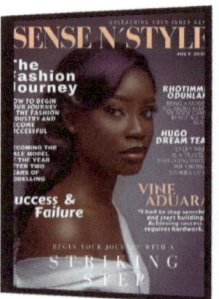
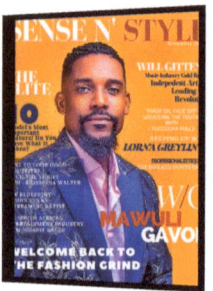
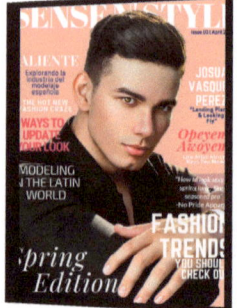
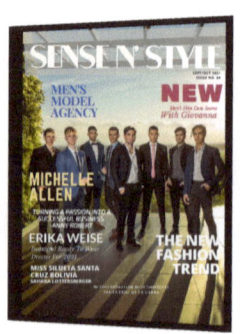
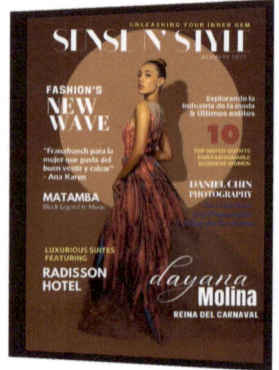

Sense N' Style Magazine has established itself as a vibrant and influential voice in the fashion industry, consistently showcasing diverse styles, emerging trends, and inspiring stories from around the globe.

Founded by Vine Aduara, who also serves as the Editor-in-Chief, and supported by a dedicated team including staff writers; Michelle Ngarama, Effie Odhiambo, the magazine has quickly become a go-to source for fashion enthusiasts and industry professionals alike.

From its inception, Sense N' Style has aimed to empower and inspire by sharing success stories of individuals within the fashion industry. Each edition is carefully structured to present a wide array of content, ranging from style inspirations to deep dives into the journeys of fashion entrepreneurs.

The magazine's mission is to provide a platform for models, designers, and young entrepreneurs, guiding them on how to navigate their paths to success with positivity and resilience.

The magazine has worked with a multitude of talented individuals across its various editions. The sixth edition, for instance, featured Kelly Chase from the Netflix show "Love Is Blind" on the cover, focusing on fashion icons, style inspiration, and entrepreneurial journeys. Other editions have spotlighted influential figures such as Quaina Watson, a top broker in Atlanta, emphasizing her remarkable journey to success.

Sense N' Style Magazine doesn't just limit itself to fashion; it delves into related industries as well.

For example, our fourth edition incorporated content on luxurious hotels, blending fashion with lifestyle and travel, and offering readers a holistic view of the stylish life. This edition highlighted how different models, entrepreneurs, and designers from various countries, especially within the Latin industry, maneuver through the fashion world in their unique contexts.

The magazine's digital and print versions ensure that fashion news, latest styles, and inspiring stories are accessible to a wide audience.

By featuring a mix of exclusive interviews, creative photoshoots, and practical advice, Sense N' Style continues to redefine how fashion content is consumed and appreciated.

In conclusion, Sense N' Style Magazine stands out not only for its fashion-forward content but also for its commitment to highlighting the personal stories and professional journeys of those within the industry. It is a testament to the power of fashion as a means of self-expression and cultural storytelling, making it an indispensable read for anyone passionate about style and innovation.

> "Our Magazine disseminates fashion news, latest styles, inspiring stories and current trends to our readers".

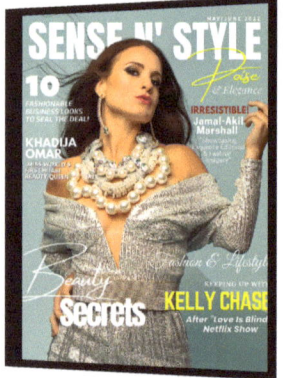
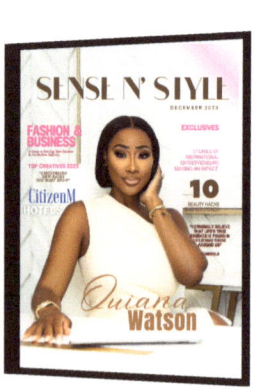
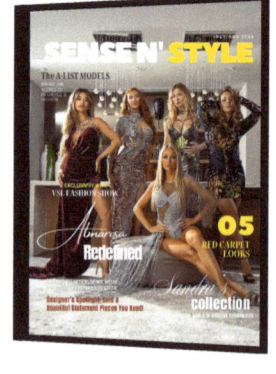
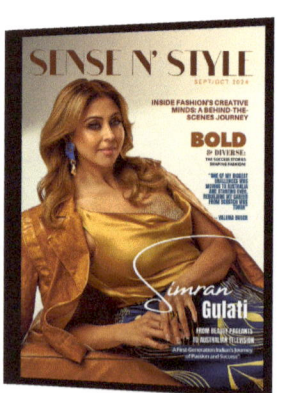

from the EDITOR

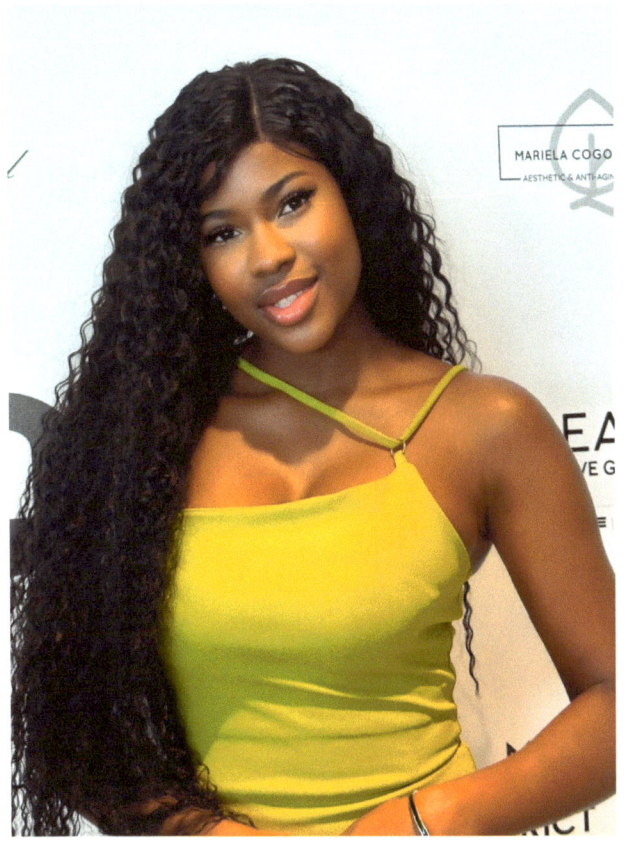

> "I remember what it felt like releasing our first edition, four years later and it still feels magical...."

SENSE N' STYLE MAGAZINE
ISSUE NO: 10

Our magazine is dedicated to showcasing the unique journeys of individuals in the fashion industry. We highlight their incredible stories, creative endeavors, and collaborations with businesses from various fields to bring a rich and diverse perspective to our readers. Over the years, we've consistently delivered inspiring content, and this issue is no exception.

This edition features Ines Trocchia on the cover, a well renowned Italian model with over 1.7 million followers who is leaving her mark in the industry. From her small town beginnings in Italy to gracing the pages of Vogue and working with top brands like Dolce & Gabbana, we delve into her inspiring journey and share her path to success. Additionally, this issue offers exclusive interviews from previous editions and engaging new articles to keep readers captivated. As a special highlight, our 10th Edition celebrates the achievements of women in 2024, showcasing their growing impact and leadership across various industries. With the stories and insights from fashion and beyond, this edition is packed with compelling content that reflects the very best of creativity and empowerment. We hope you enjoy this exciting read!

Vine Aduara

FOUNDER| EDITOR IN CHIEF
Sense N' Style Magazine

About Our Founder

Vine Oghenekparobo Aduara, holding a degree in Criminal Law, is not only a legal professional but also an accomplished model with a rich work experience with various brands, companies, agencies, and designers. As the founder of VI-Models, an academy dedicated to modeling development, and the brain behind Sense N' Style Magazine, Vine is a spectacular entrepreneur with diverse talents. Driven by a vision to mentor and guide aspiring entrepreneurs, Vine Aduara aspires to offer the best platform to anyone embarking on their professional journeys across various career paths.

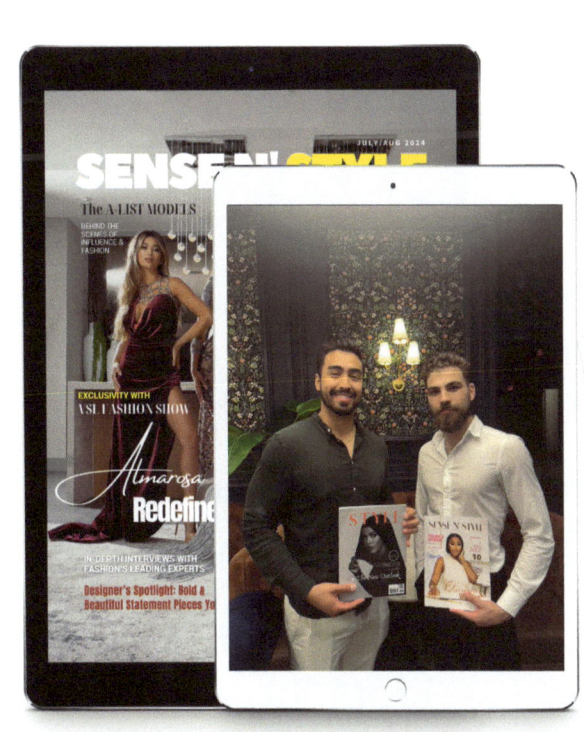

SEASON GREETINGS!

The Christmas Holiday Inspo

Whatever your style is, the key is feeling good while looking great. Whether you choose to stick to classic Christmas colors, go for a more minimalist approach, or embrace the glitz and glam of the season, make sure that whatever you wear makes you feel confident and ready to enjoy the holidays to the fullest.

Photographed by Daniel Chin for Creardent SCZ

> SEASON GREETINGS!

The Holiday Fashion

Switch it up for the best time of the year!

Choosing the right outfit for the holiday season!

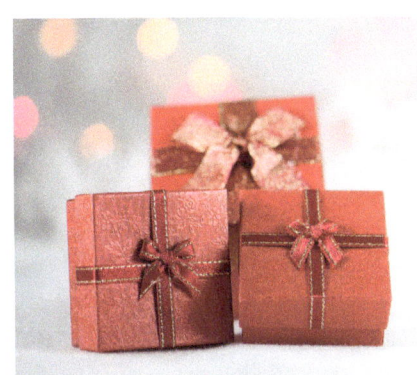

As the Christmas season rolls in, it's the perfect time to get creative with your wardrobe and embrace the festive spirit. Dressing up for the holidays doesn't mean you have to go all out with glitter and sequins unless that's your style. It's all about mixing comfort with a touch of celebration, and with a little planning, you can nail the Christmas look without breaking the bank.

Start with the basics: A cozy sweater is always a great place to begin. If you're heading to a family gathering or a casual holiday event, opt for a festive yet understated design. Think classic red or green hues, or even a plaid pattern. You don't need to wear something overly flashy to look stylish. For instance, a sweater paired with a comfy pair of jeans is an effortless look that can work for almost any occasion.

Although, if you're dressing up for a more formal Christmas dinner or work party, you might want to put on something a bit more elegant.

> FOR THOSE HOLIDAY GET TOGETHERS WHERE EVERYONE'S A LITTLE MORE LAID BACK, YOU CAN ALWAYS ROCK A CASUAL LOOK WITH A TWIST!

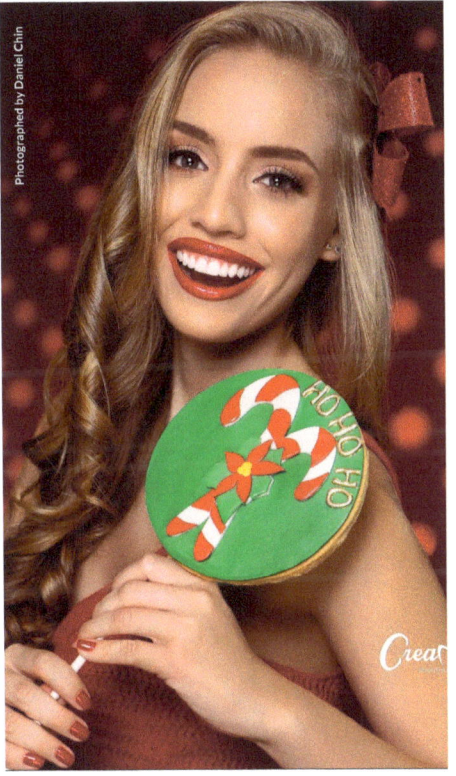

Photographed by Daniel Chin

In general, ladies can go for a simple velvet dress, which is cozy and festive without feeling too over-the-top. Add a pair of simple heels or boots, and you've got a refined yet comfortable outfit. On the other hand, men can easily wear a fitted blazer and dress trousers, with or without a tie depending on the event's formality.

A nice button-up shirt under the blazer, with maybe a pop of color like a burgundy or forest green, will give you a sophisticated but approachable vibe. For those holiday get togethers where everyone's a little more laid back, you can always rock a casual look with a twist. Think oversized sweaters paired with leggings or even leather pants. This is an easy way to stay warm while keeping it stylish. If you want to add some Christmas flair, throw in some holiday themed accessories. For example, a chunky scarf in festive colors or a cute beanie adds just enough personality without feeling too much.

Most importantly, don't forget your accessories. Christmas jewelry, like a pair of gold or silver hoop earrings, or a fun snowflake necklace, can bring both playful and chic to your outfit. For footwear, ankle boots or simple ballet flats can be both fashionable and comfortable for running around during the busy holiday season.

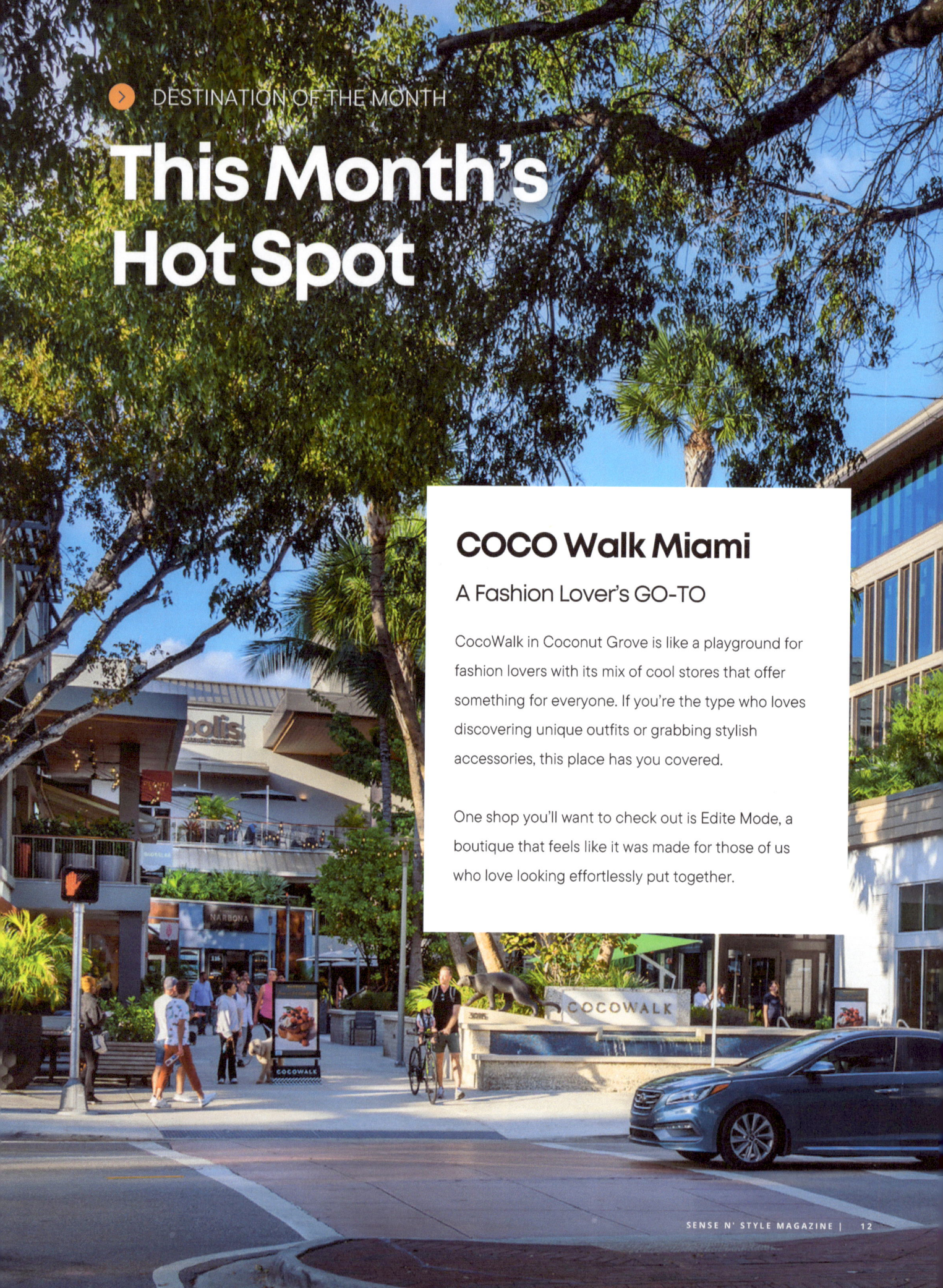

› DESTINATION OF THE MONTH

This Month's Hot Spot

COCO Walk Miami

A Fashion Lover's GO-TO

CocoWalk in Coconut Grove is like a playground for fashion lovers with its mix of cool stores that offer something for everyone. If you're the type who loves discovering unique outfits or grabbing stylish accessories, this place has you covered.

One shop you'll want to check out is Edite Mode, a boutique that feels like it was made for those of us who love looking effortlessly put together.

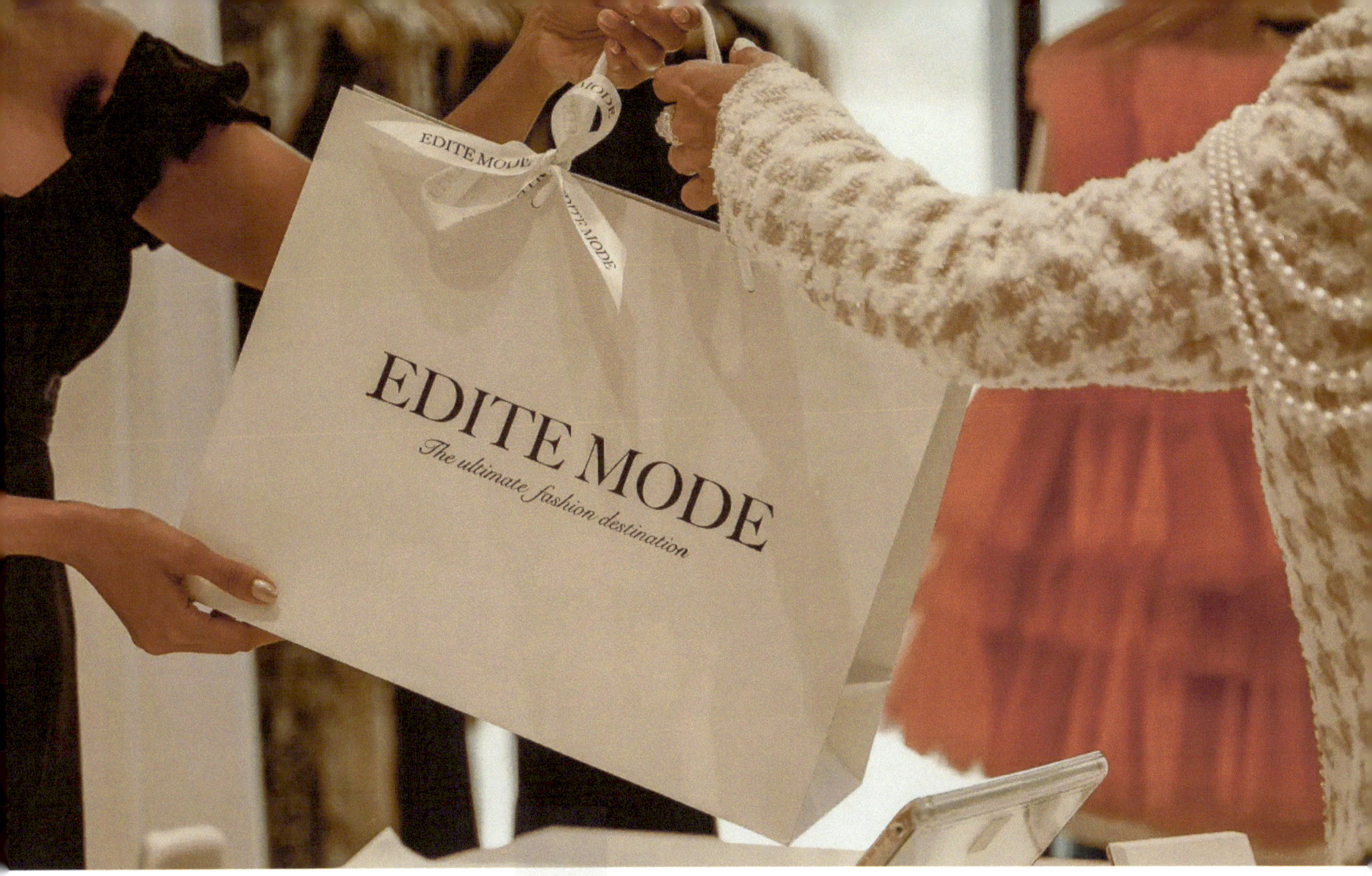

EDITE MODE

You'll find everything from cozy cardigans to eye catching dresses that are perfect for a night out or even a fancy event.

Oh, and their accessories? You'll probably want to leave with more than you planned. Custom painted shoes and necklaces that add just the right amount of flair to any outfit. Right next door, they've got a shoe shop that's equally tempting, with everything from fashionable heels to comfy flats. If you're into jewelry that makes a statement, Gas Bijoux is like a little treasure chest. They have earrings, bracelets, and necklaces that look like art pieces you'd want to show off. It's the kind of stuff that makes any outfit pop, whether you're dressing up for a party or just elevating a casual look.

For those days when you want to feel sporty but still stylish, there's FP Movement. It's all about activewear that transitions from yoga class to grabbing a smoothie with friends. Think leggings and tops that are comfortable and trendy at the same time.

What makes CocoWalk even better is the vibe, it's not just about shopping. You can grab a bite, sip on coffee, or even catch a movie after you're done exploring the stores. The whole experience feels laid back yet upscale, which is very Miami.

So, if you're in the mood to refresh your wardrobe or just want a fun day out in style, CocoWalk is the spot. You'll walk away feeling inspired and probably with a few shopping bags in hand!

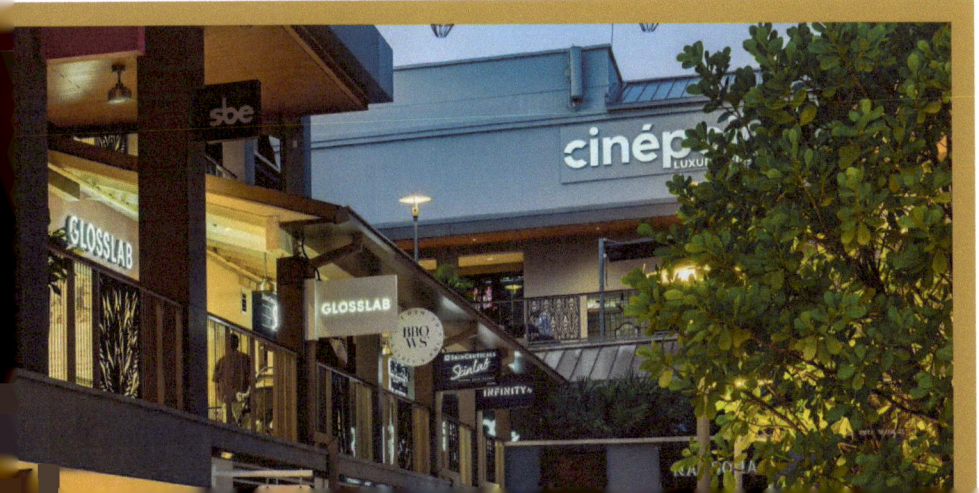

ISSUE NO. 10

ANNY ROBERT

EXCLUSIVE INTERVIEW 'HIGHLIGHT'

Read full article on our website www.sensenstyle.com

SCAN TO CONTACT

Editorial PORTRAITS

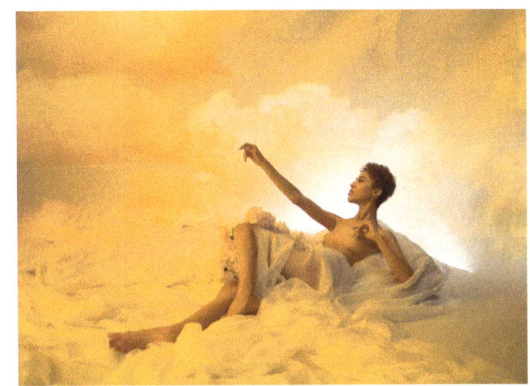

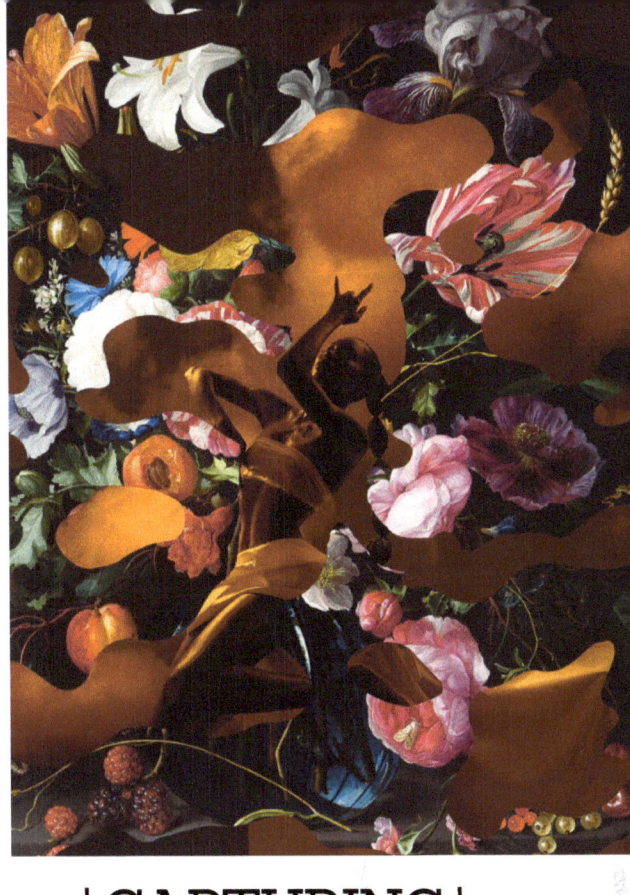

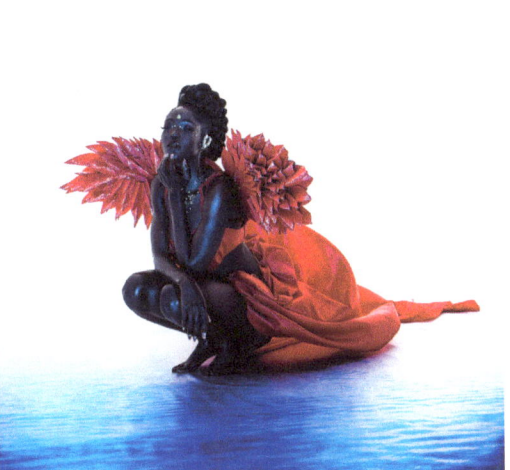

'CAPTURING' UNIQUE MOMENTS

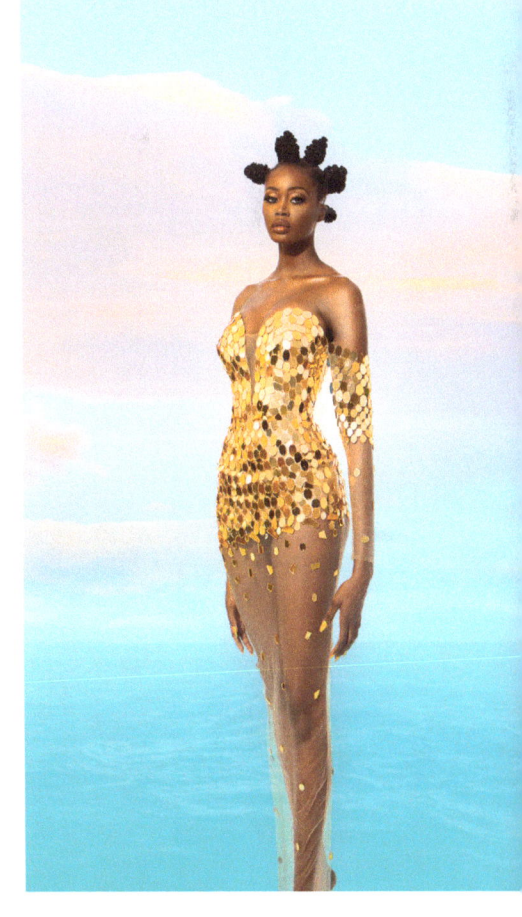

AS A PHOTOGRAPHER, WHAT IS YOUR CREATIVE PROCESS LIKE?

My creative process is based on research. I go through a lot of photos everyday to make sure I have the inspiration saved for things I want to do. I get bits of inspiration from different creations and then create something unique. My process is based on what I see as well. For instance I can't look at models too much when I have a photoshoot for a family portrait. So I constantly have to look at different ideas because I work with different people.

ADVICE TO ASPIRING PHOTOGRAPHERS LOOKING TO GET INTO THE INDUSTRY

Art does not always kick start successfully, it takes a while before you start seeing results, so it is important to have something that you do at the side. I did something similar, I was employed with a company while still learning photography, I still had my safety net and I only resigned when I knew my passion would be sustainable. I feel like people should not downplay the role of money in life. Whatever your outlook on life is, money still controls what you eat, wear and it's a basic necessity so it's important to have it. The second thing is to try not to put pressure on yourself. Although when I started, my rise was pretty fast because I was already into graphic design for about 7 years so that was similar to what I ventured into. However, you must understand your niche and avoid putting pressure on yourself.

Creatively always push yourself, however when it comes to the result, take it easy on yourself and take things carefully. Lastly, avoid too many people criticizing your work.

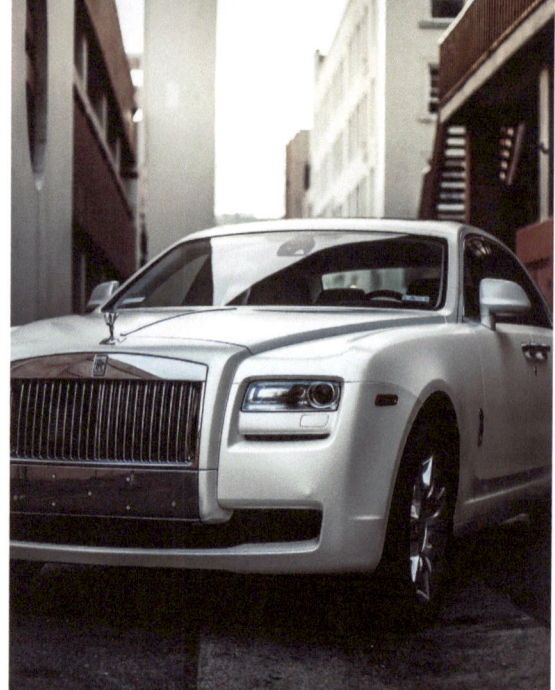
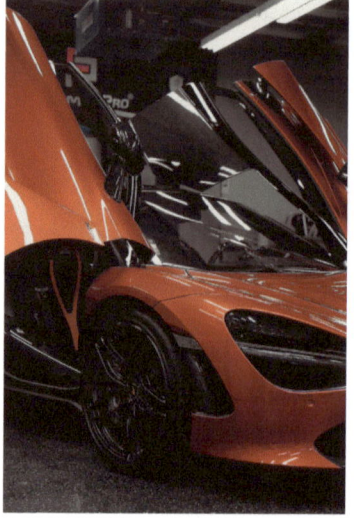

An Exclusive Review

SCAN FOR CONTACT

THE NEW LUXURY

IF YOU'RE SOMEONE WHO BELIEVES YOUR CAR SHOULD MATCH YOUR VIBE, CERTAIN MODELS STAND OUT AS A TRUE FASHION STATEMENTS.

Dream cars and fashion have always been intertwined. The cars we dream of owning often say as much about our style as the clothes we wear. They are not just vehicles but expressions of identity, showcasing personality, ambition, and flair in the same way a signature outfit does.

Imagine driving a Rolls-Royce, the ultimate symbol of elegance and luxury. It's not just a car; it's an experience. The design and interiors feel like stepping into a perfectly made outfit where everything fits just right, and every detail speaks of sophistication. If your style leans toward classic looks with a timeless appeal, this car is like wearing a black tie to every event.

On the flip side, you have the Lamborghini. Picture its sharp lines and colors like lime green or electric yellow, it's impossible not to turn heads. Driving one feels like strutting down a runway in a bold statement piece that screams confidence. It's the car for someone unafraid to stand out, someone whose wardrobe is filled with eye catching outfits and daring accessories.

For those who prefer a minimalist approach, a Tesla makes perfect sense. Its design and focus on sustainability align with modern fashion trends of clean lines and ethical choices. Driving a Tesla is like dressing in a chic, all neutral outfit effortlessly cool yet intentional.

Then there's the charm of a Jeep Wrangler. If your style leans towards boho chic or adventurous looks, this car is your perfect match. It's like wearing a denim jacket and boots, casual, versatile, and ready for any adventure. It tells the world you're laid back but always ready to hit the road.

Some cars, like the Porsche 911, mix retro vibes with modern appeal. Driving one feels like rocking vintage fashion with a twist, one can say its a statement that never goes out of style. Its smooth curves and iconic design are perfect for someone who loves the old school look with today's trends.

If practicality and luxury are your priorities, the Range Rover fits the bill. It's like power dressing, a mix of functionality and elegance. You can feel equally comfortable pulling up to a glamorous event or tackling a busy day. It's the car for someone who values substance as much as style.

For those who love to stay ahead of the curve, a futuristic car like the Mercedes-Benz EQS is the way to go. With its almost sci-fi-like design, it complements a wardrobe. It's the car for someone always looking forward, experimenting with trends, and setting the pace.

As we conclude, I'd say dream cars are more than just machines, they're part of how we express ourselves. Just like a great outfit, the right car can make you feel unstoppable, capturing your essence in a way words often can't. Whether you're drawn to classic style, statements pieces , or minimalistic, there's a dream car that fits your style. After all, life is your runway, and the car you drive is the ultimate accessory.

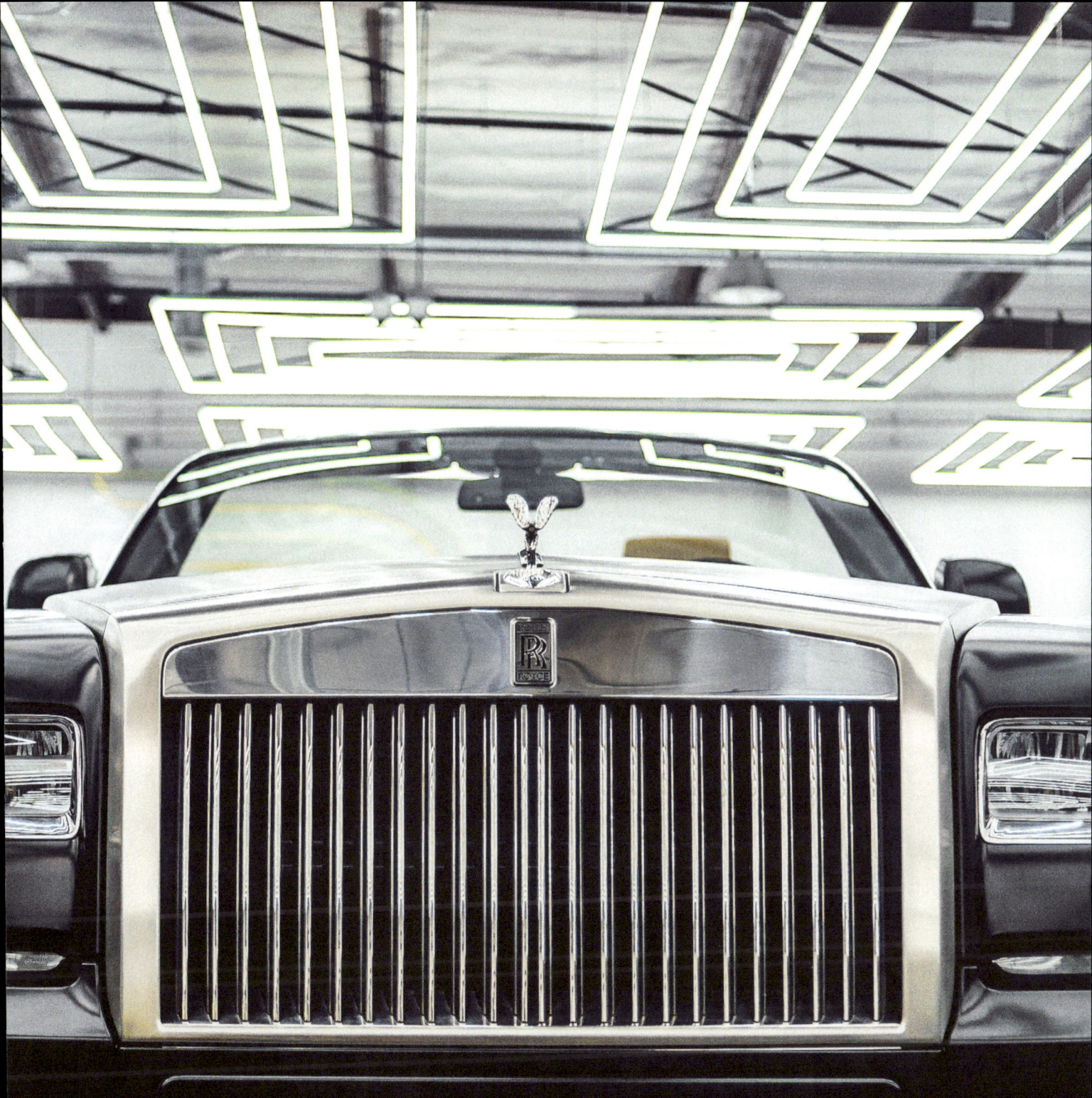

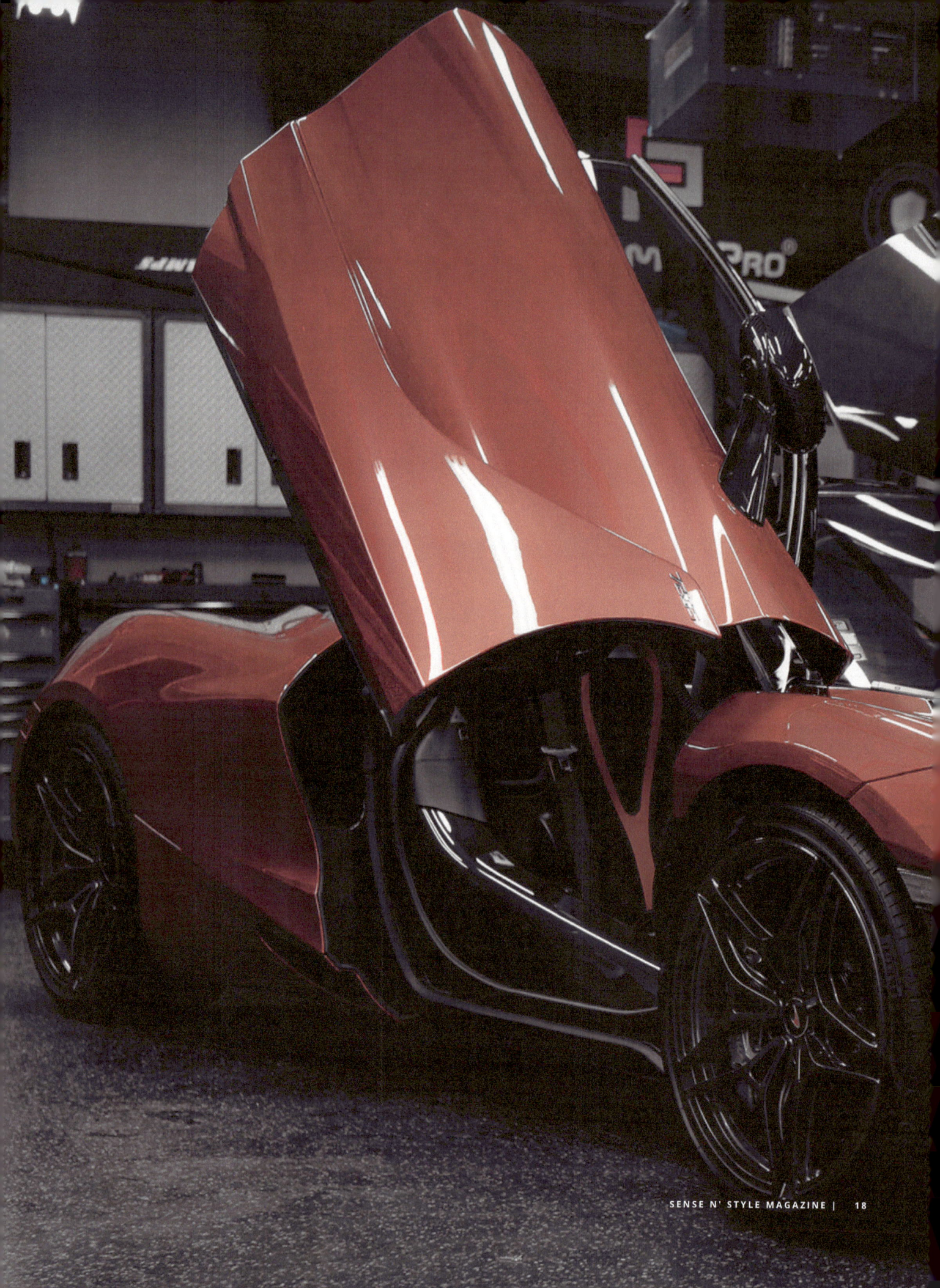

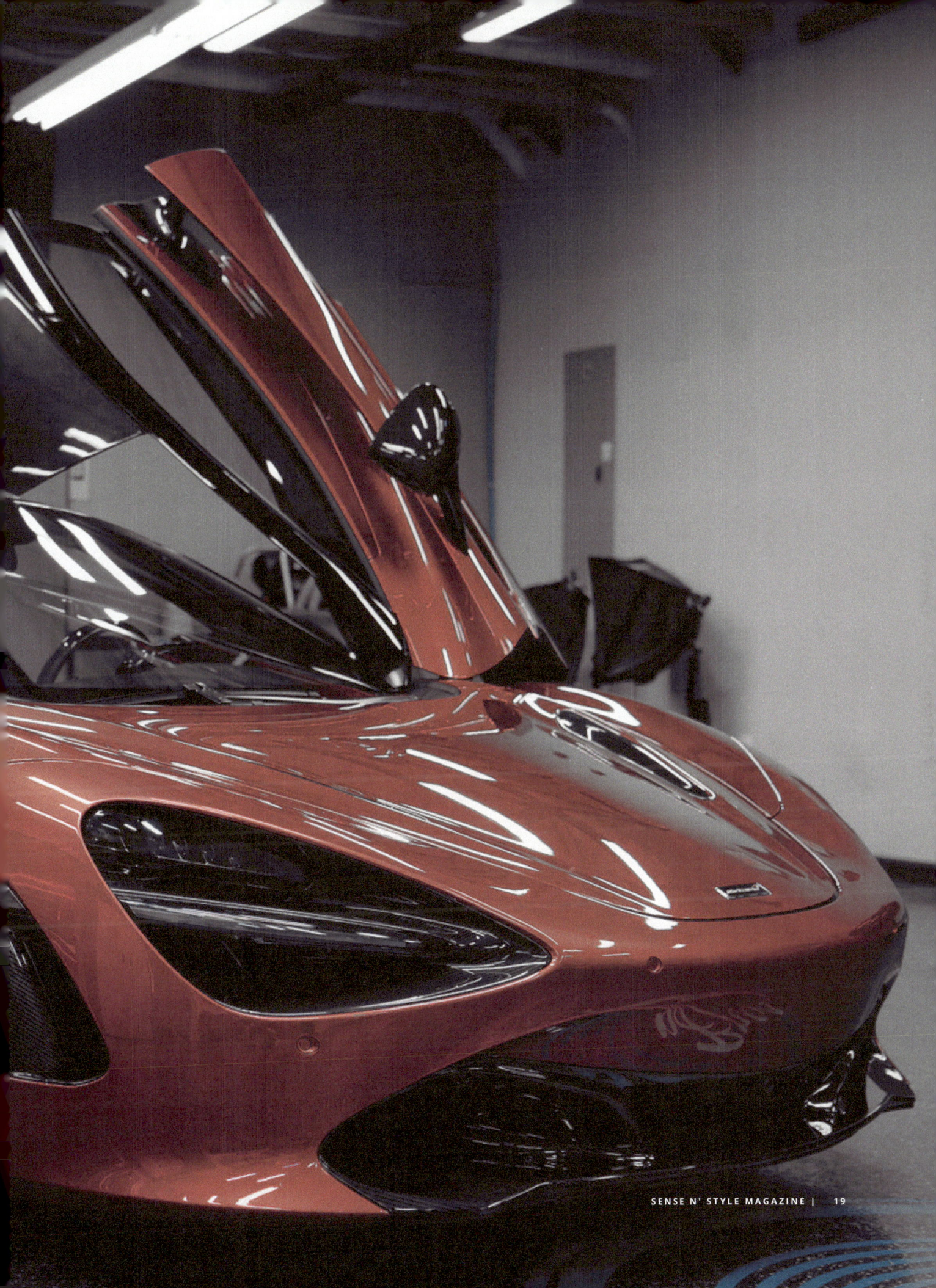

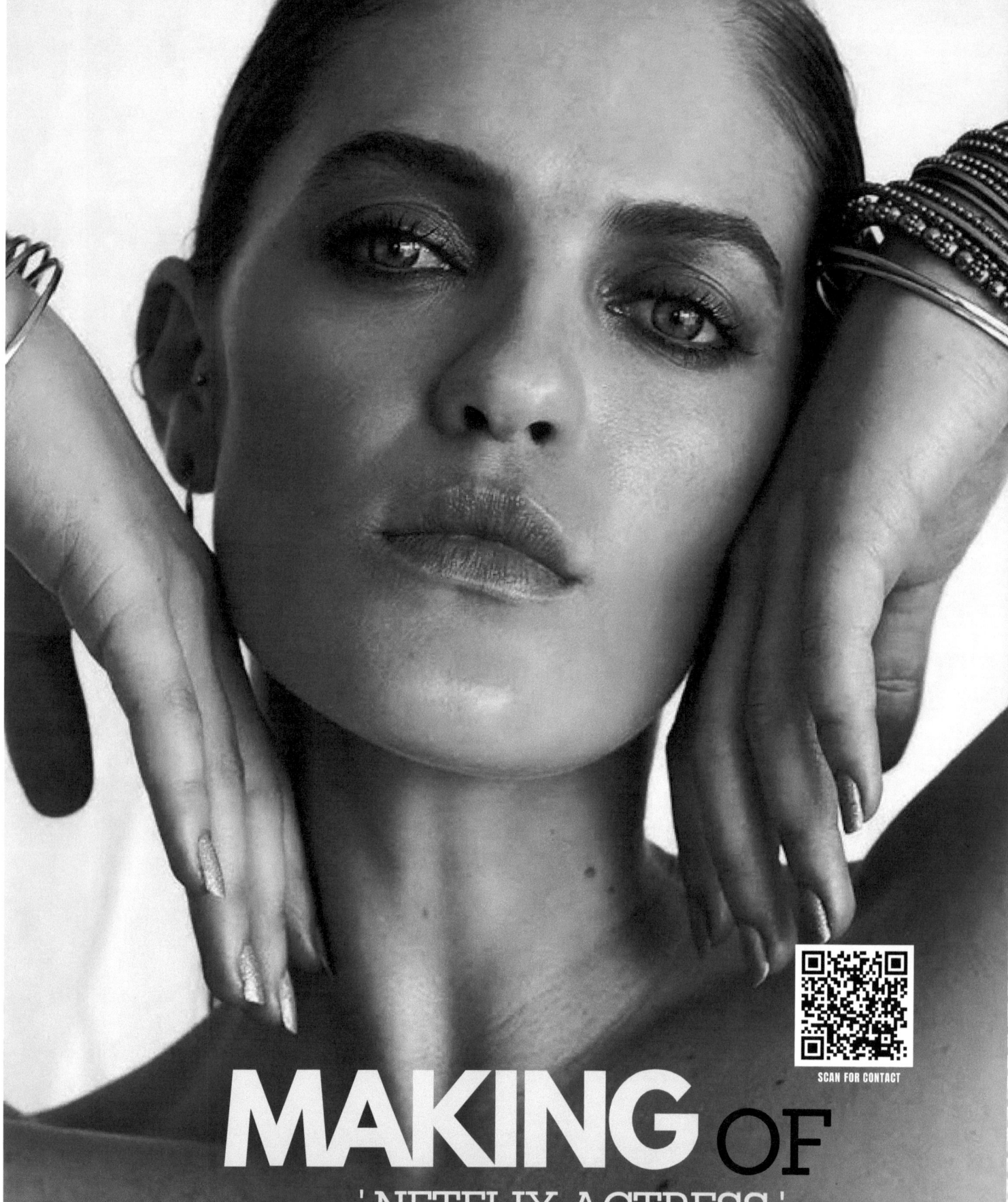

MAKING OF
'NETFLIX ACTRESS'
MICHELLE ALLEN

Photographed by Vaughan Treyvellan

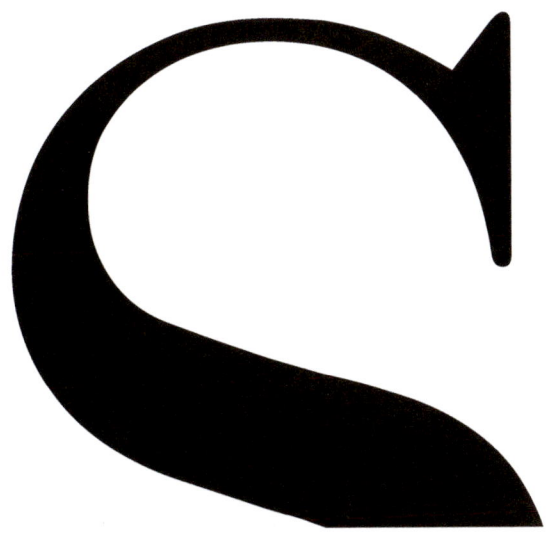

KINDLY TELL US ABOUT YOURSELF

For starters; I grew up on a farm in South Africa and eventually moved to Cape Town. So I've always been slightly more reserved, as moving around a lot made me comfortable with being alone. Perhaps that triggered my need for creativity as I was always wandering around & asking questions about my environment.

WHAT ARE YOU MOST PASSIONATE ABOUT?

Creation! In all formats. I really just love life. Which has been a journey in itself. Falling in love with being alive fuels everything I would like to accomplish. I've become somewhat of a seeker in this lifetime and grasping philosophical and esoteric texts really excite me as I truly believe these go hand in hand with creation

HOW HAS YOUR JOURNEY IN THE FASHION & ENTERTAINMENT INDUSTRY BEEN SO FAR?

The experience has been amazing. There have of course been some sour tasting moments but in retrospect I really needed them to grow as an individual, which in turn just gave more depth to what else I have to offer within the industry.

I used to get so caught up in comparing myself to others. I was even in a well known modeling competition, and those kinds of environments are a breeding ground for toxic behaviour within this industry. Im so grateful for that experience as I learnt so much but I doubt I'll ever be apart of / promote a competition again. Due to this, i took a really long break from it all. I actually went to live in India for a few months by myself. Being away from everything and everyone I knew, really made me get to know myself again; and that's exactly what I do now

I'm into aliens and going to the cinema by myself. I collect crystals and once went to a casting with wet hair. I am the only one that is with me forever, so why would I care if you like me or not. If whatever you're aiming for is a match to you, it'll be yours. Choose yourself. Always.

WHAT IS THE GREATEST THING YOU'D WANT TO ACCOMPLISH IN THE ENTERTAINMENT INDUSTRY?

I just want to keeping creating for me. To be part of new stories that I care about, and have people enjoy/be inspired by what I have to offer

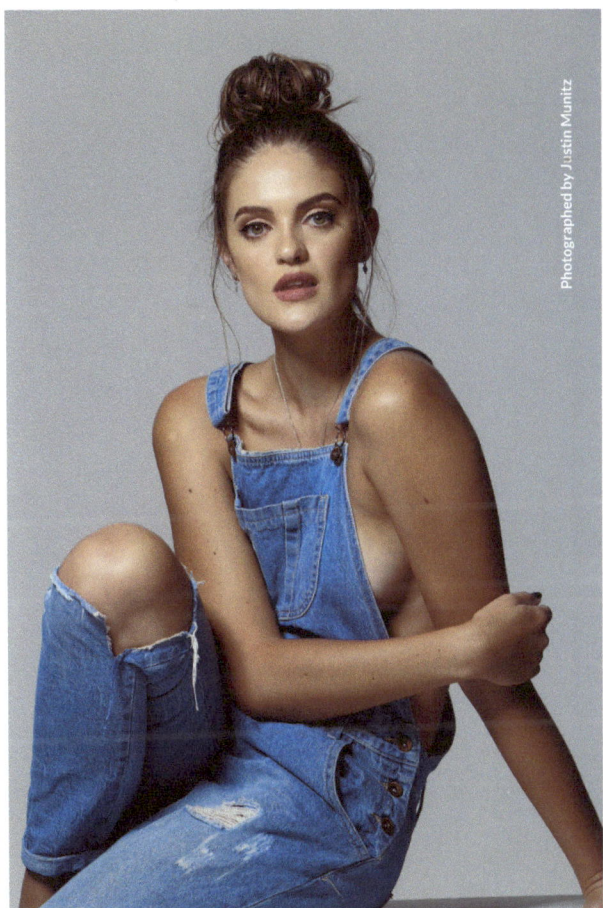

Photographed by Justin Munitz

> "I used to get so caught up in comparing myself to others. I was even in a well known modeling competition, and those kinds of environments are a breeding ground for toxic behavior within this industry."
>
> —MICHELLE ALLEN

THE JOURNEY
An exclusive interview

TELL US ABOUT HOW YOU STARTED YOUR JOURNEY IN THE ACTING INDUSTRY AS WELL AS THE MODELING INDUSTRY.

I always took part in the drama shows in school and even did some small pageants as a young teen. I guess like most actors - the concept of becoming someone else was very intriguing.

I love to watch people; from how someone walks to how they eat. So being able to embody something other than my already organic way of emoting triggered me to step into acting. .

Production Team:
Model: Ines Trocchia
Photographer: Richard Berryman
Styled by: Daniel Alamillo
Make up Artist: Eva Glez

SCAN FOR CONTACT

EXPLORING
THE FACE BEHIND THE COVER

THE INSIDER LOOK

What scares me more is settling for less, not getting what I want out of life, or feeling like I didn't give my best effort to achieve my goals. My desire to succeed was much stronger than any fear of failure.

MODEL @INESTROCCHIA
PH @WHATSHISFACEDO
STYLE @DANIELALAMILLO_
MUA @EVAGLEZBEAUTY

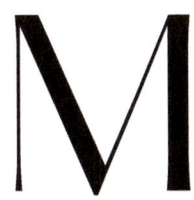

My name is Ines Trocchia, I am originally from a very small town in southern Italy. My upbringing was simple and grounded, with a strong emphasis on family values. I received a good education, but my environment was very conservative.

People from my town often viewed ambitious dreams as unrealistic, favoring more traditional, secure career paths. So when I started modeling at 17, I made the bold decision to move to Milan at 18 on my own. Initially, my family wasn't supportive; they didn't believe in modeling as a viable career option. But I trusted my instincts, took a leap of faith, and looking back, it was one of the best decisions I've ever made.

What are you most passionate about?

I love a lot of things, but I'm especially passionate about what I do. That's the key, choosing something you truly enjoy and are skilled at. When your job aligns with your passion, it doesn't feel like work. For me, it's the opposite; it's exciting and motivating. I don't feel weighed down by work; instead, I feel sad or bored when I don't have enough to do. I also have a deep love for art, photography, and architecture, which I believe ties beautifully into the beauty and fashion industry

You moved to Milan at 18, coming from a small town, what motivated you to make that bold move at such a young age?

I'd say I was never really scared of failure. Now that I'm a little older, things might feel a bit different, but at that time, I wasn't afraid of failing. Even now, to a certain extent, I'm still not. What scares me more is settling for less, not getting what I want out of life, or feeling like I didn't give my best effort to achieve my goals. My desire to succeed was much stronger than any fear of failure.

What would you say were some of the pivotal moments that shaped your path?

I feel like I had a steady, progressive journey, but if I had to pinpoint a moment that truly shaped my career, it would be when I was 21 and started working for an Italian TV program about sports. From that point on, a lot of opportunities began to open up for me. I got involved in interviews, podcasts, and radio, which helped increase both my exposure and my following. This period, from ages 21 to 24, was pivotal in solidifying my career path.

You got your big break early on, starting in television work from 21-24 years old, including working with Italian soccer and on a radio podcast. Can you share what this experience was like for you and what it taught you?

Honestly, it was amazing because it was the first time I got to show a bit of my personality, even though it was a sports program, which was, of course, quite serious. However, after that, I had the opportunity to work on a much more entertaining show. I never expected my life to take that turn, but it did, and I found myself loving television. I loved how it allowed people to feel more connected to me, but I don't think I was fully prepared for it.

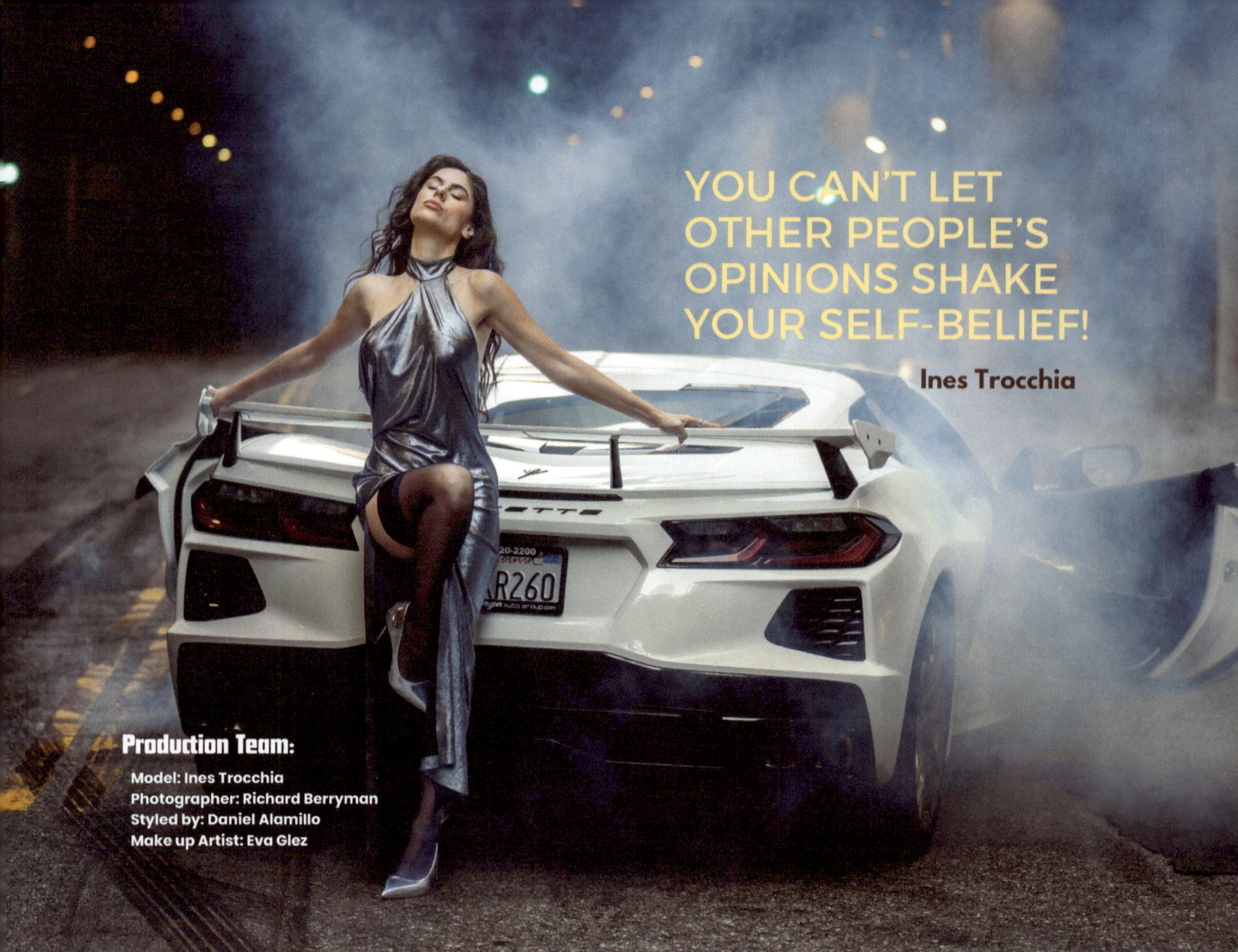

YOU CAN'T LET OTHER PEOPLE'S OPINIONS SHAKE YOUR SELF-BELIEF!

Ines Trocchia

Production Team:
Model: Ines Trocchia
Photographer: Richard Berryman
Styled by: Daniel Alamillo
Make up Artist: Eva Glez

CAN YOU SHARE A MEMORABLE HIGH POINT IN YOUR PHOTOGRAPHY CAREER AND WHAT IT MEANT TO YOU?

The first time I was on television, I was overwhelmed by all the lights and was extremely nervous. Looking back, I wish I had more guidance during that time. My family wasn't involved in the fashion or entertainment industries, and I didn't have anyone close to me who could provide advice.

There weren't many trustworthy people in the industry either, so I often felt lost. I was a 21-year-old girl with so much to figure out in a competitive and complex business.

WHEN COVID HIT AND ITALY WENT INTO LOCKDOWN, YOU BEGAN FOCUSING ON SOCIAL MEDIA, GROWING YOUR AUDIENCE TO 1.7 MILLION FOLLOWERS FROM HALF A MILLION. WHAT WAS YOUR STRATEGY BEHIND CREATING AN INTERNATIONAL AUDIENCE?

I just started sharing more about myself and my life. I don't have a secret formula; I guess I simply put out content that resonated with people. That's just who I am. Honestly, I don't think I had any special strategy, it was more about being consistent and authentic

WHAT ARE SOME CHALLENGES YOU'VE FACED IN THE MODELING INDUSTRY

One of the biggest challenges for me was my height. These days, the industry embraces diversity, and there are many successful models who are shorter.

However, I am 5'7", and back when I started, it was really difficult because there were very few models of my height in the industry. Another major challenge was dealing with rejection. You have to be very strong and confident in yourself.

You can't let other people's opinions shake your self-belief because this industry often makes you feel like you're not enough. It's essential to remind yourself that you are enough. Of course, you should always strive to improve, but you must avoid falling into the trap of changing yourself too much.

I also had to come to terms with the fact that nothing comes easy in this business. There are always comparisons, and you'll see plenty of other girls who look amazing. This is why self-confidence is so important. You need to handle rejection, keep trying, and remind yourself that you're worth it. With so many beautiful girls competing alongside you, being confident in your uniqueness is the key.

HOW HAVE YOU BEEN ABLE TO OVERCOME THESE CHALLENGES

I think the answer is determination in both cases, because I knew I had great strength and a good sense of proportion. I was hardworking, disciplined, and knew how to pose. Even though I was aware of my flaws and knew there were certain things I couldn't reach, I also knew I had valuable skills. I was determined to prove that I was worth it.

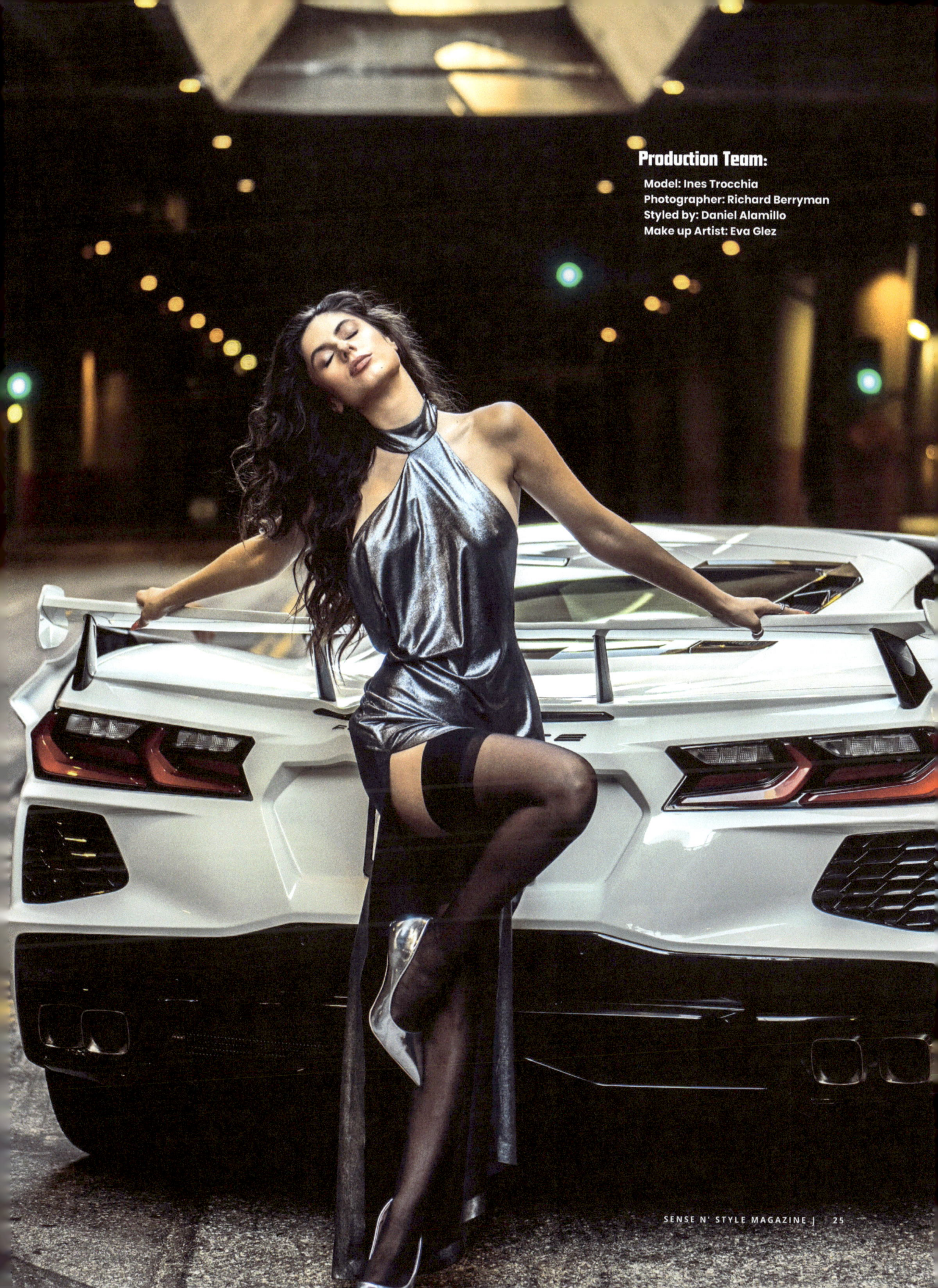

THE journey

Fashion & Style

OUT OF ALL YOUR ACHIEVEMENTS, WHICH ONE STANDS OUT AS A CAREER HIGHLIGHT?

Landing the cover of *Vogue* was a dream come true. It's one of my proudest accomplishments.

YOU'VE MODELED FOR HIGH-PROFILE BRANDS LIKE DOLCE & GABBANA, ROBERTO CAVALLI, AND PHILIPP PLEIN. HOW HAS WORKING WITH THESE ICONIC BRANDS SHAPED YOUR CAREER?

I loved it; I think these brands perfectly match my personality. I always believe it's important to find your niche and identify the brands that enhance your qualities, as well as those you can elevate. What's the perfect match? Not every brand works for everyone, and it's crucial to find a style that suits you. I love brands that enhance femininity, beauty, sensuality, sexuality, and the concept of a strong woman who isn't afraid to embrace her sex appeal. It's a natural outcome based on your appearance and energy.

I naturally come across as a confident woman, and I'm happy to represent brands that celebrate and enhance women's sensuality

WHAT ADVICE WOULD YOU GIVE TO UPCOMING MODELS WHO ASPIRE TO BREAK INTO THE INDUSTRY?

There are a few pieces of advice I'd give. The first is to not give up. You need to work hard because nothing comes quickly, so don't get discouraged by the first closed door. You need to keep going and believe in yourself because success takes time to build. The second piece of advice is to find your niche and focus on something you're good at that sets you apart from others.

The third is to be your true self and not feel like you need to conform to a certain stereotype or adapt to trends. I believe the biggest difference between you and someone else is you—the way you move, the way you talk. So, embrace and improve your true self. Enhance who you are, but never feel like you have to change to fit into a particular category.

> " I always believe it's important to find your niche and identify the brands that enhance your qualities, as well as those you can elevate."
> — Ines Trocchia

KINDLY TELL US ABOUT YOUR DRESSING STYLE - WHAT IS YOUR GO TO OUTFIT

It depends on the occasion. During the day, when I'm running errands, my style is very simple, nothing elaborate, no makeup, and a bit sporty. If I have to go out, I think my style is more sexy. I love brands that enhance my beauty and exude sexiness, but with class. I'm not afraid to show my femininity. There are so many brands like the ones I mentioned before, such as Versace and Balmain, which embody the idea of a sexy, empowered woman.

ANY RECENT FASHION OBSESSIONS?

Honestly, it might sound a bit strange, but I love skim dresses. I know they're very basic, but I'm collecting them in different colors. However, if we're talking about something more sophisticated, I'd say I like the classy boss-lady office style. They are quite masculine, yet still revealing and sexy, which really gives off a 'boss lady' vibe.

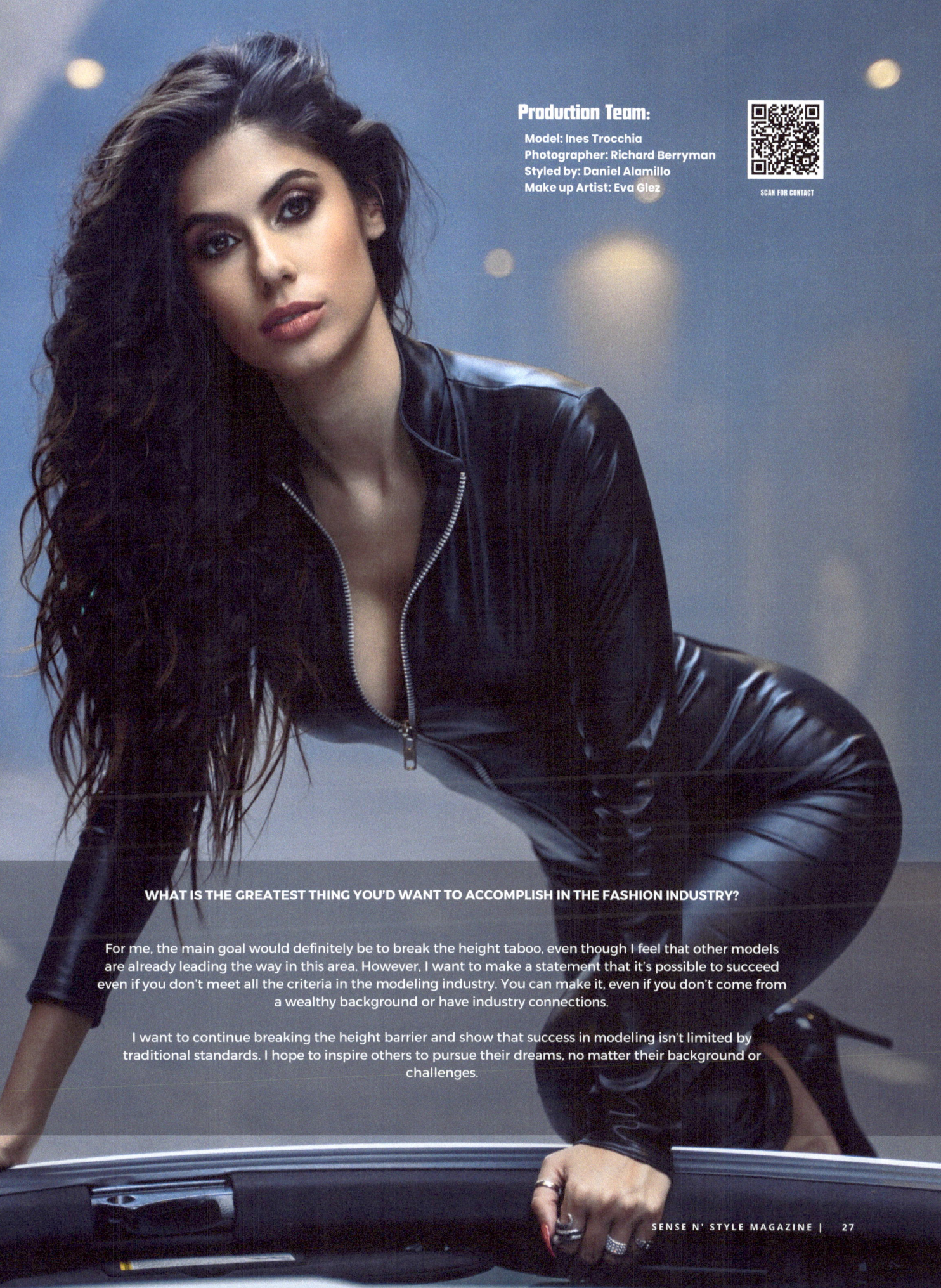

Production Team:
Model: Ines Trocchia
Photographer: Richard Berryman
Styled by: Daniel Alamillo
Make up Artist: Eva Glez

SCAN FOR CONTACT

WHAT IS THE GREATEST THING YOU'D WANT TO ACCOMPLISH IN THE FASHION INDUSTRY?

For me, the main goal would definitely be to break the height taboo, even though I feel that other models are already leading the way in this area. However, I want to make a statement that it's possible to succeed even if you don't meet all the criteria in the modeling industry. You can make it, even if you don't come from a wealthy background or have industry connections.

I want to continue breaking the height barrier and show that success in modeling isn't limited by traditional standards. I hope to inspire others to pursue their dreams, no matter their background or challenges.

SKINCARE

A GUIDE TO SELF LOVE

Sense N' Style Magazine Special

I never thought much about skincare. To me, it always felt like one of those extra things people did just to be trendy or because they had too much free time. I'd see shelves of products at stores or hear friends talking about their routines and think, Do I really need all that? My mornings were rushed especially because of work, and the idea of adding one more step felt unnecessary.

I was fine with a quick splash of water and whatever moisturizer I had lying around. It worked, or at least I thought it did.

But then, life got a little chaotic. Between work, personal commitments, and the general rush of everyday life, I realized I rarely made time for myself. I wasn't just neglecting my skin, I was overlooking moments to pause and care for me.

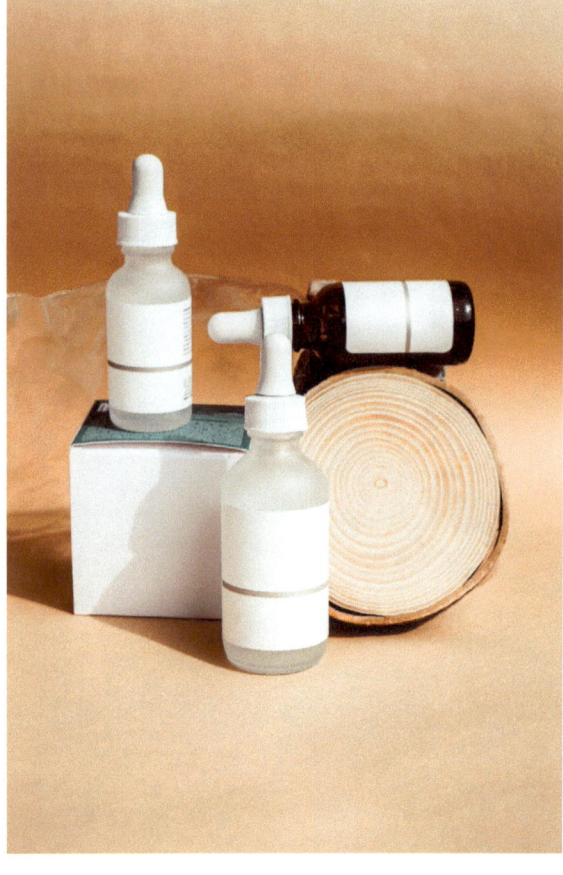

The first time I truly spent time on a skincare routine, it felt strange. It wasn't glamorous or picture perfect. I stood in front of the mirror, hesitating over how much cleanser to use and awkwardly patting my face dry. But as I repeated the process night after night, something unexpected happened. That ten or fifteen minutes of focusing on myself became my favorite part of the day.

Applying a face mask or massaging in a moisturizer wasn't just about my skin; it was about creating space to slow down, breathe, and give myself attention. I started to notice small changes in my skin, brighter, smoother, healthier looking. But more than that, I felt more connected to myself.

That time in front of the mirror became a quiet moment to reflect, think, or simply exist without distractions.

My skin started to show signs of stress. A few breakouts here, dryness there, and the dullness that seemed to echo how I felt inside. It was then that I decided to give skincare a real try, not just for beauty reasons but as a form of self-care

It felt like I was nourishing more than my skin; I was nourishing my soul. Every step, from cleansing to hydrating, felt like a little act of love for myself.

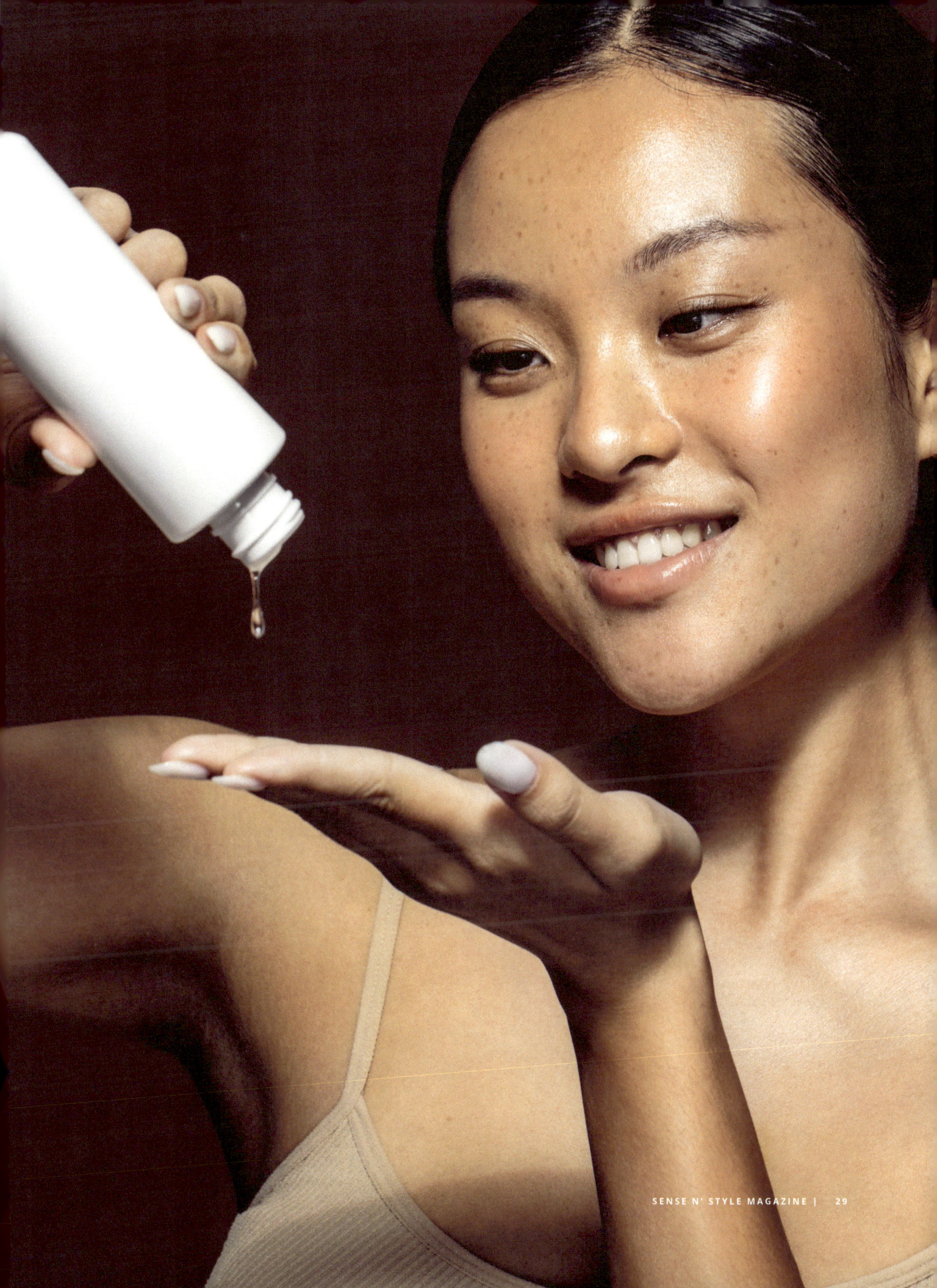

T

SKINCARE ISN'T JUST ABOUT LOOKING GOOD, IT'S ABOUT FEELING GOOD, TREATING YOURSELF WITH KINDNESS, AND BUILDING A STRONGER CONNECTION TO WHO YOU ARE

The Editor's Special · Sense N' Style Magazine

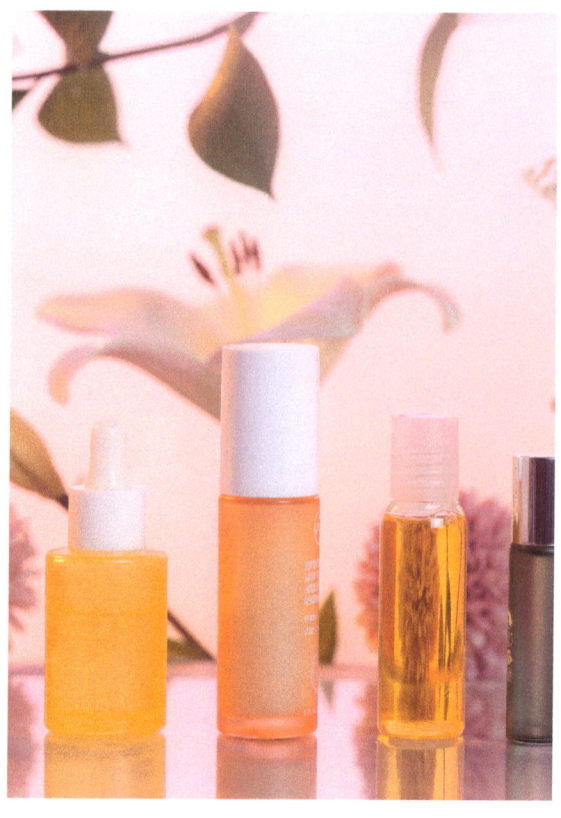

What surprised me the most was how this small change started to ripple into other areas of my life. I started prioritizing more moments of self-care, whether it was reading, journaling, or simply saying no to things that didn't serve me. I realized that self-love isn't always about big, dramatic gestures, it can be found in small, consistent acts, like taking care of your skin.

Looking back, I think I avoided skincare because I didn't think I deserved to spend time on something so "extra." But now, I see it differently. Taking care of myself isn't extra; it's essential.

Skincare became my guide to loving myself, one step at a time. It taught me to appreciate the time I spend with myself and the effort I put into my well being.

It's funny how something I once dismissed as unnecessary became one of the most grounding parts of my day. Now, I look forward to my skincare routine, not just for the benefits it brings to my skin but for the peace it brings to my mind. It's a daily reminder that I'm worth the time and care I give myself.

Skincare isn't just about looking good, it's about feeling good, treating yourself with kindness, and building a stronger connection to who you are.

It may have started with a cleanser and a moisturizer, but it turned into something much deeper: a ritual of self love.

APPLYING A FACE MASK OR MASSAGING IN A MOISTURIZER ISN'T JUST ABOUT YOUR SKIN; IT'S ABOUT CREATING SPACE TO SLOW DOWN, BREATHE, AND GIVE YOURSELF ATTENTION

That time in front of the mirror becomes a quiet moment to reflect, think, or simply exist without distractions.

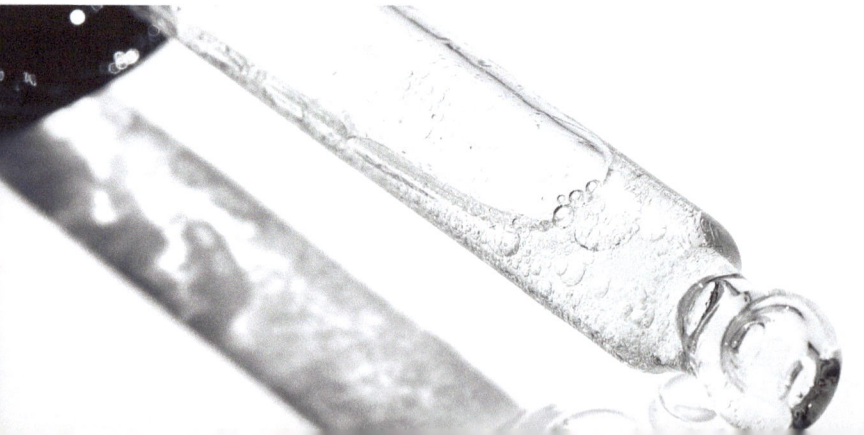

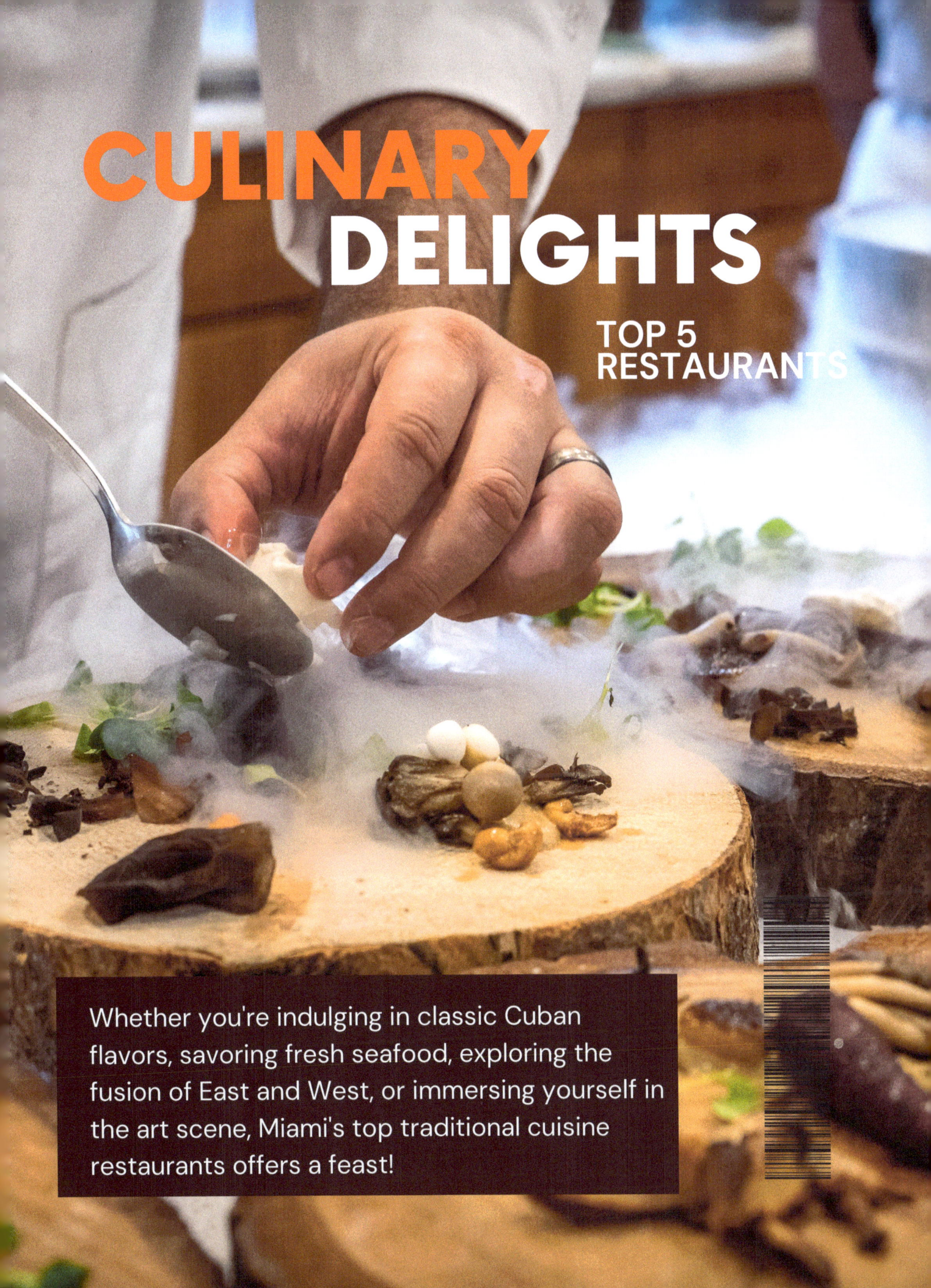

CULINARY DELIGHTS

TOP 5 RESTAURANTS

Whether you're indulging in classic Cuban flavors, savoring fresh seafood, exploring the fusion of East and West, or immersing yourself in the art scene, Miami's top traditional cuisine restaurants offers a feast!

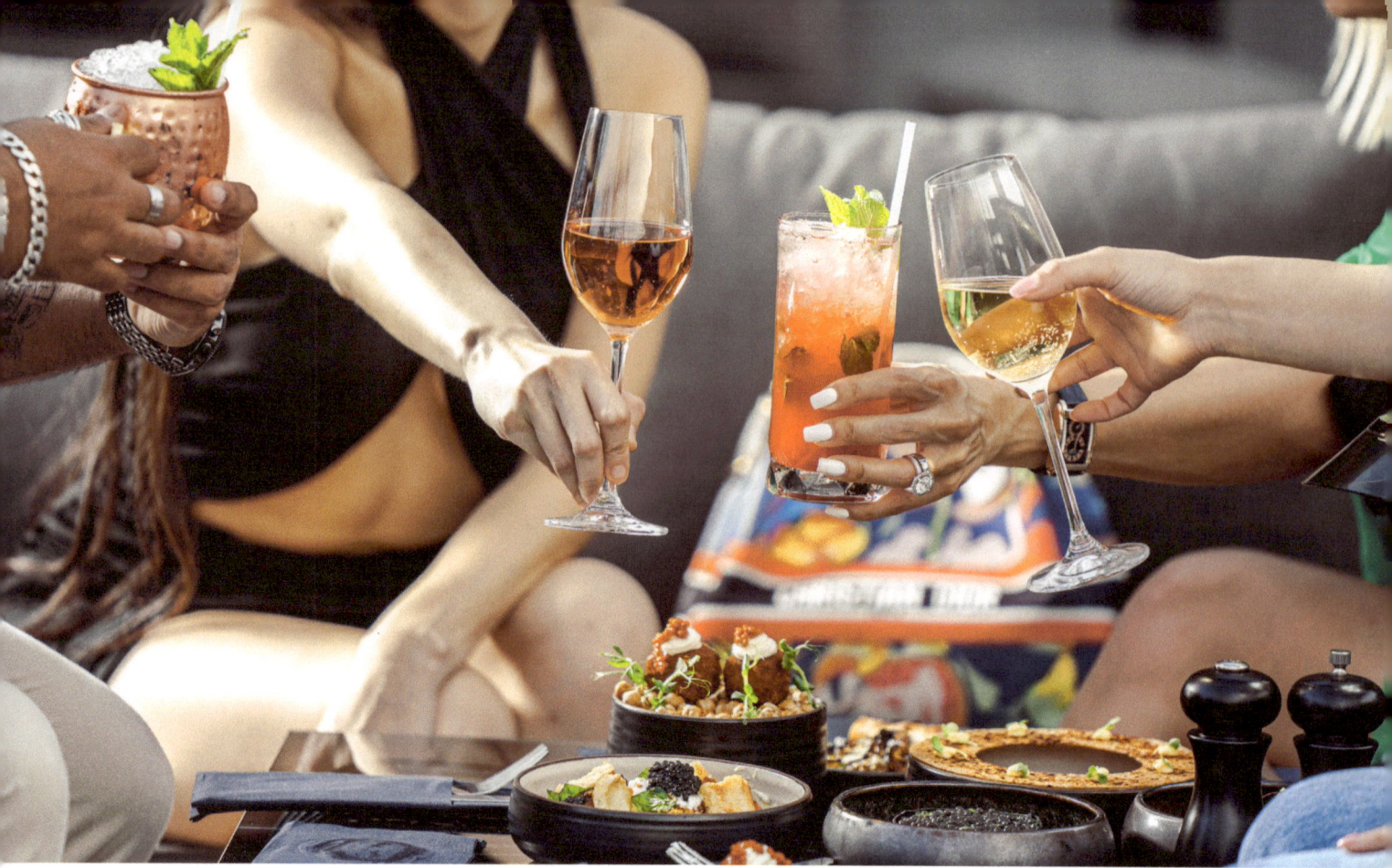

Miami, a city known for its culture, beautiful beaches, and exciting nightlife, also boasts diverse restaurants. From fresh seafood to Latin-inspired flavors, Miami's top restaurants serving cultural dishes takes you on a journey that reflects the city's rich diversity. Let's explore some of the top dining establishments that contribute to Miami's reputation as a food lover's paradise.

Versailles Restaurant – A Taste of Cuba in Little Havana

No exploration of Miami's dinning is complete without a visit to Little Havana, and at the heart of this cultural hub lies Versailles Restaurant. Known as an iconic Cuban eatery, Versailles has been serving up authentic Cuban cuisine since 1971. From classic Cuban sandwiches to savory picadillo, this restaurant captures the essence of Havana, making it a must-visit for those seeking an authentic taste of Cuba in Miami.

Joe's Stone Crab – A Seafood Institution

For over a century, Joe's Stone Crab has been a beacon of excellence in Miami's seafood scene. Located in the historic Art Deco district of South Beach, Joe's is renowned for its signature stone crab claws, a delicacy that draws locals and visitors alike. The elegant yet laid-back atmosphere, combined with impeccable service, makes Joe's Stone Crab a destination for those seeking the freshest seafood in Miami

A JOURNEY WORTH SAVORING!

CULINARY DELIGHTS
YOUR GO-TO SPOTS

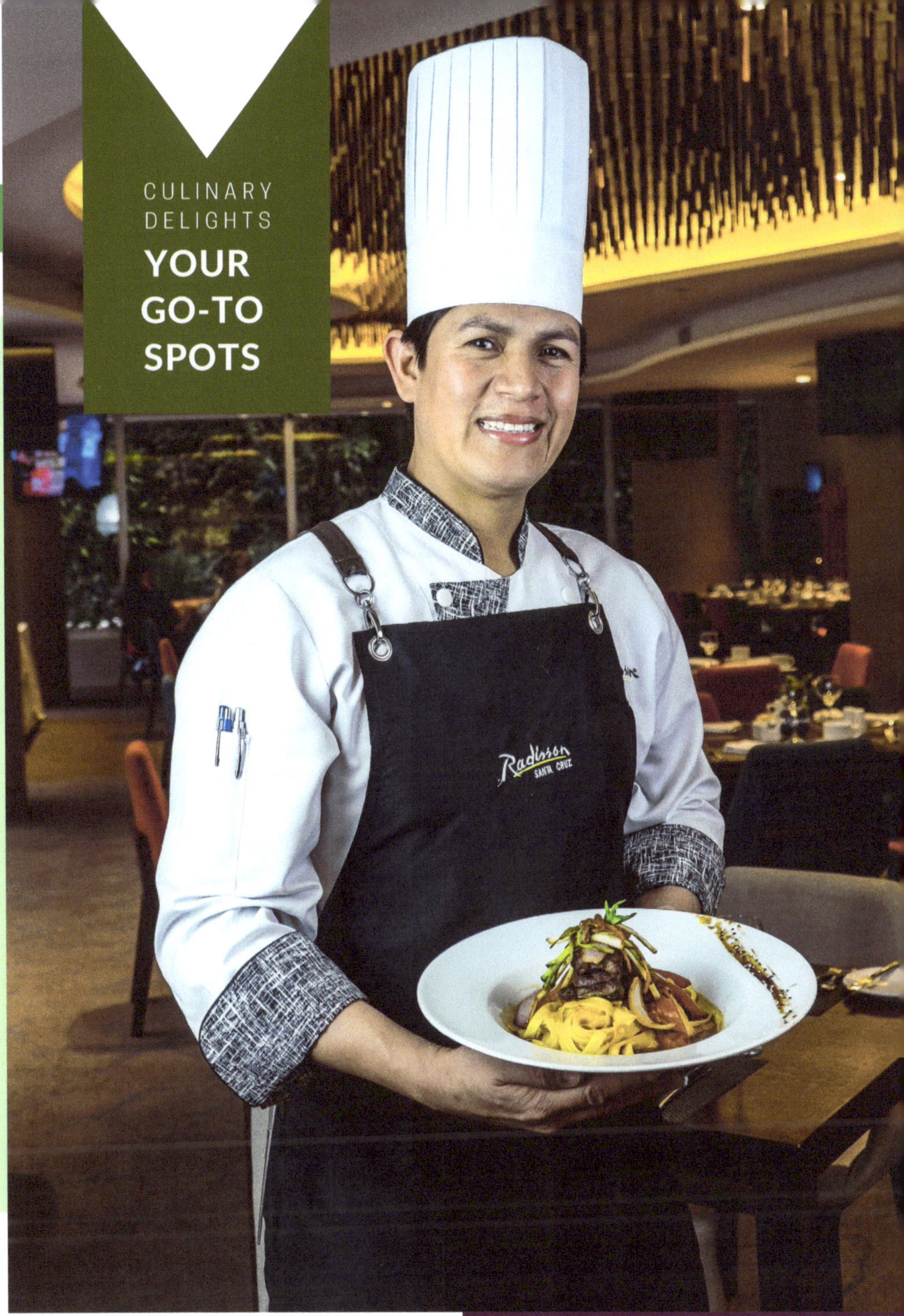

Komodo – Where East Meets Miami Chic

For a taste of Asian flavors and Miami's trendy vibe, Komodo stands out as a gem.

This upscale restaurant in the heart of Brickell has the Eastern and Western influences, offering a menu that features everything from dim sum to sushi. With its stylish setting and rooftop lounge' breathtaking views of the city skyline, Komodo is not just a dining experience; it's a celebration of amazing dishes coming together.

Wynwood Kitchen & Bar – Art and Gastronomy Collide

Wynwood, known for its vibrant street art and creative energy, is home to Wynwood Kitchen & Bar, a restaurant that integrates art into its services.

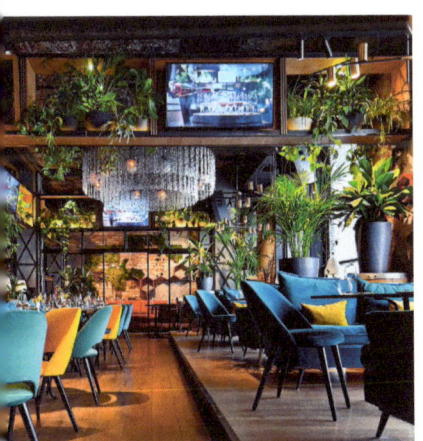

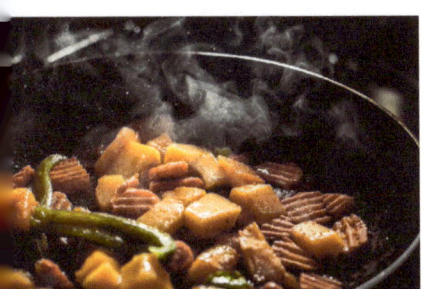

This trendy establishment offers a diverse menu inspired by Latin and global flavors, with dishes that are as visually appealing. Wynwood Kitchen & Bar provides a dining experience where art and different cultures come together

Zuma – Japanese Izakaya

Dining with a Miami Twist in the heart of downtown Miami, Zuma brings the art of izakaya dining to the Magic City.

This Japanese restaurant offers a sophisticated yet laid-back atmosphere where guests can savor a variety of dishes from the robata grill, sushi, and sashimi. With its waterfront location and a menu that highlights the best of Japanese cuisine, Zuma has become a go-to destination for those seeking a modern and refined dining experience in Miami.

The various restaurants in Miami is a testament to the city's diversity and creativity. Whether you're indulging in classic Cuban flavors, savoring fresh seafood, exploring the fusion of East and West, or in the art scene, Miami's top restaurants offer a feast for the senses.

As a melting pot of cultures and cuisines, the city continues to evolve, ensuring that every restaurant in Miami is a journey worth savoring.

QADIRA
FIND THE LATEST HAUTE COUTURE DESIGNERS HERE

Production Team
Designs: QADIRA
Photographed by: Micky Angel Vargas
Make Up Artist: Leonardo Salinas
Models: Martina Alaiza
Lucia Maria
Camila Bohrt

BY GLENDA & ROLANDO

Production Team
Designs: QADIRA
Photographed by: Micky Angel Vargas
Make Up Artist: Leonardo Salinas
Models: Martina Alaiza
Lucia Maria
Camila Bohrt

THE SIGNATURE STYLE ARE THE EMBROIDERY AND THE TRANSPARENCY OF THE GARMENTS. CREATED TO ACCENTUATE EVERY CURVE OF A WOMAN'S BODY.

QADIRA HAUTE COUTURE DESIGNS

Exclusive FASHION Style

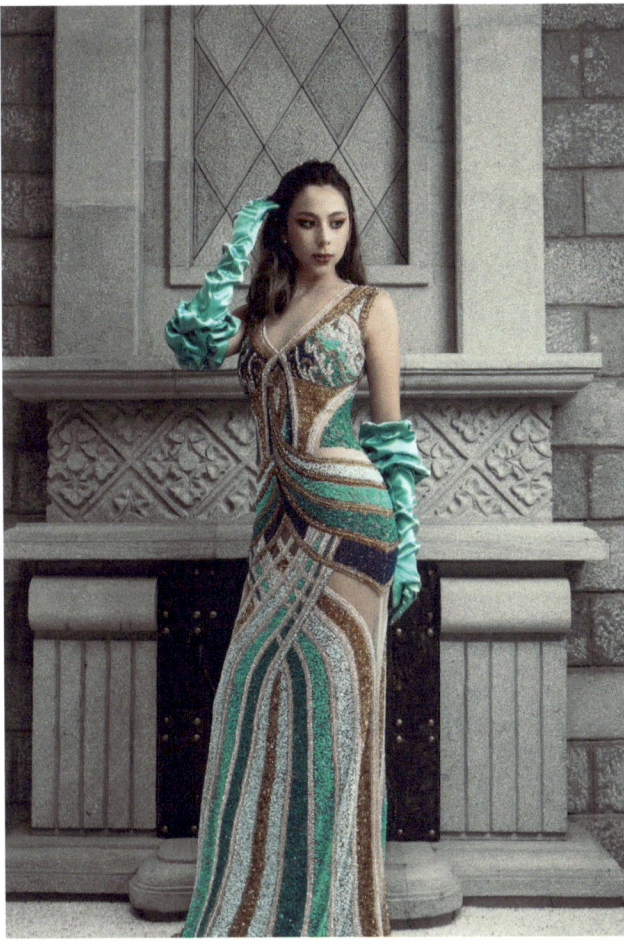

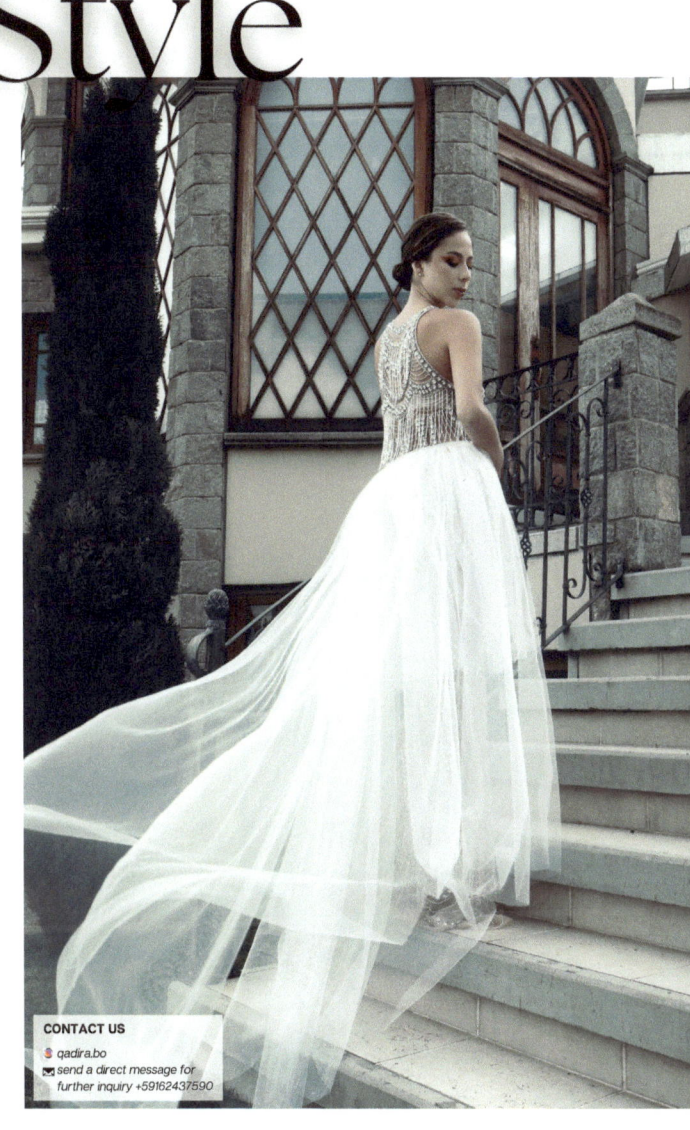

CONTACT US
qadira.bo
send a direct message for further inquiry +59162437590

BIOGRAPHY

Qadira was established in February 2021, in La Paz Bolivia by Glenda Bohrt and Rolando Canido. This brand and partnership was born from a mutual passion for fashion and friendship between co-founders.

Rolando comes from a multicultural family influenced by Lebanese and Brazilian culture. He grew up in Beni, the warm and tropical side of Bolivia known as an adventurous place full of natural beauty. During his teens he lived in Naples Florida in the USA to later on come back to Bolivia, where he went to the University in La Paz. He graduated as an Environmental Engineer and met Glenda Bohrt, a local from La Paz.

Glenda Bohrt's family was already involved in the industry of Fashion having founded Altifiber, a llama and alpaca fabric producer exporting all kinds of alpaca outwear internationally.

Glenda's mother a painter and a designer who owned a store of Alpaca outwear in one of the most prominent commercial neighborhood of La Paz.

From a young age Glenda Bohrt saw the process of design and production and carried this love for fashion during her years abroad living in Paris, London, Milan and New York.

Ironically her studies much like her partner's, Rolando, had little to do with fashion. Glenda has a bachelor's degree in international business and a double Masters Degree in Corporate Finance and Global Finance. Even if academically fashion was not the focus of their careers, they were both very involved in the industry.

Rolando was scouted during his university years and walked in the biggest fashion events of the country for major national and international designers like Custo Barcelona. He also learned about the design process of a fashion line creating his own brand for men clothing and even taught himself to sew.

During the pandemic, their friendship grew and an exchange of ideas, virtues and designs began. They sought to make something original and striking. More than a brand, they wanted people to experience something risky and elegant inspired by haute couture, but also modern and timeless like a jewel. They customize every gown for every type of body. Their signature style are the embroidery and the transparency of the garments, created to accentuate every curve of a woman's body. Like the name, the designs are influenced from the middle eastern culture and the raw materials come from the United Emirates.

Haute couture consists of secrets whispered from generation to generation, **If, in ready-to-wear, a garment is manufactured according to standard sizes,** *the haute couture garment adapts to any imperfection in order to eliminate it.*

-Yves Saint Laurent

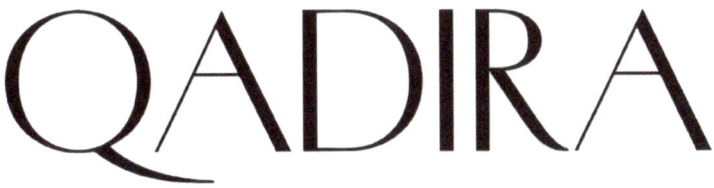

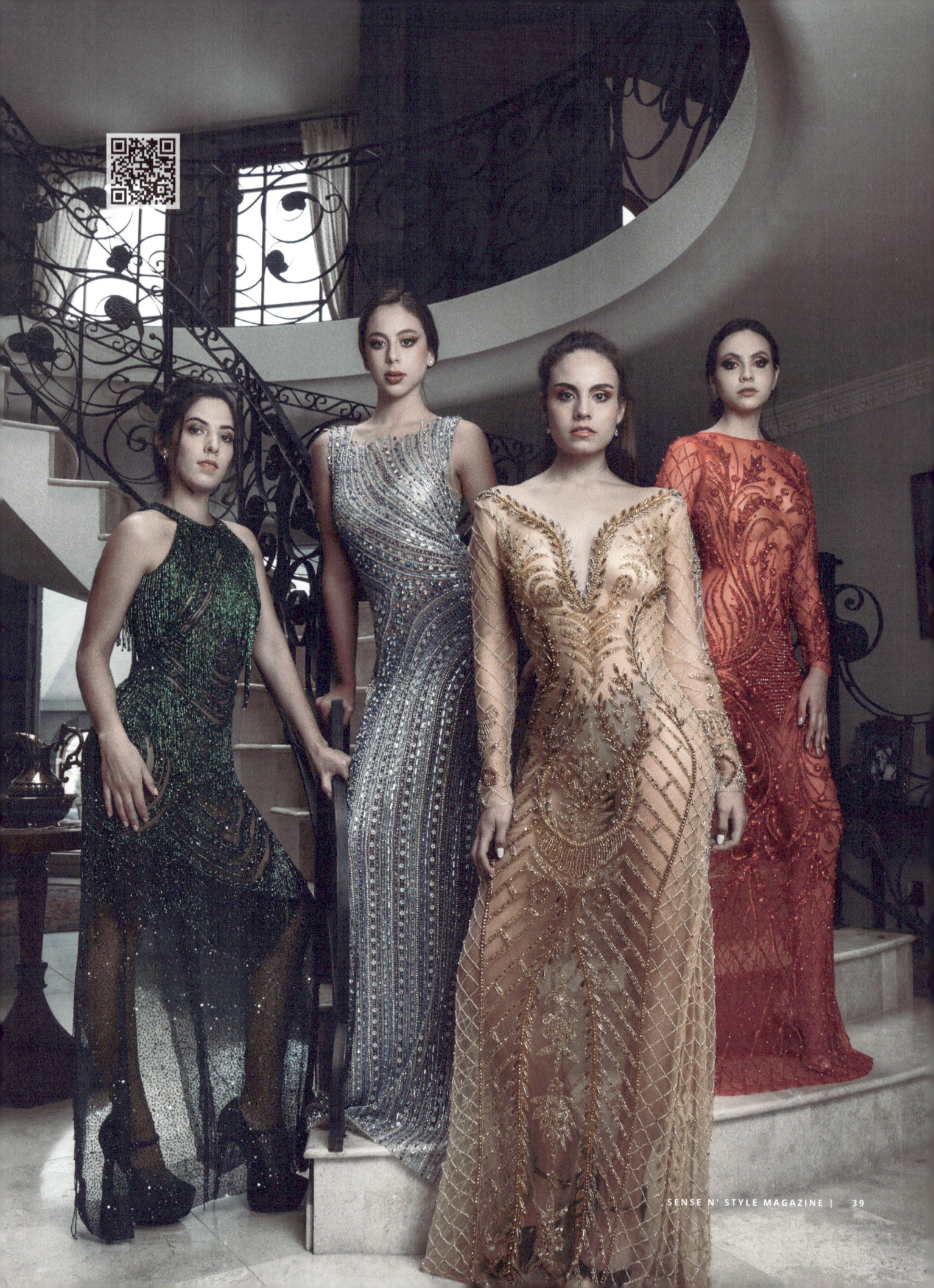

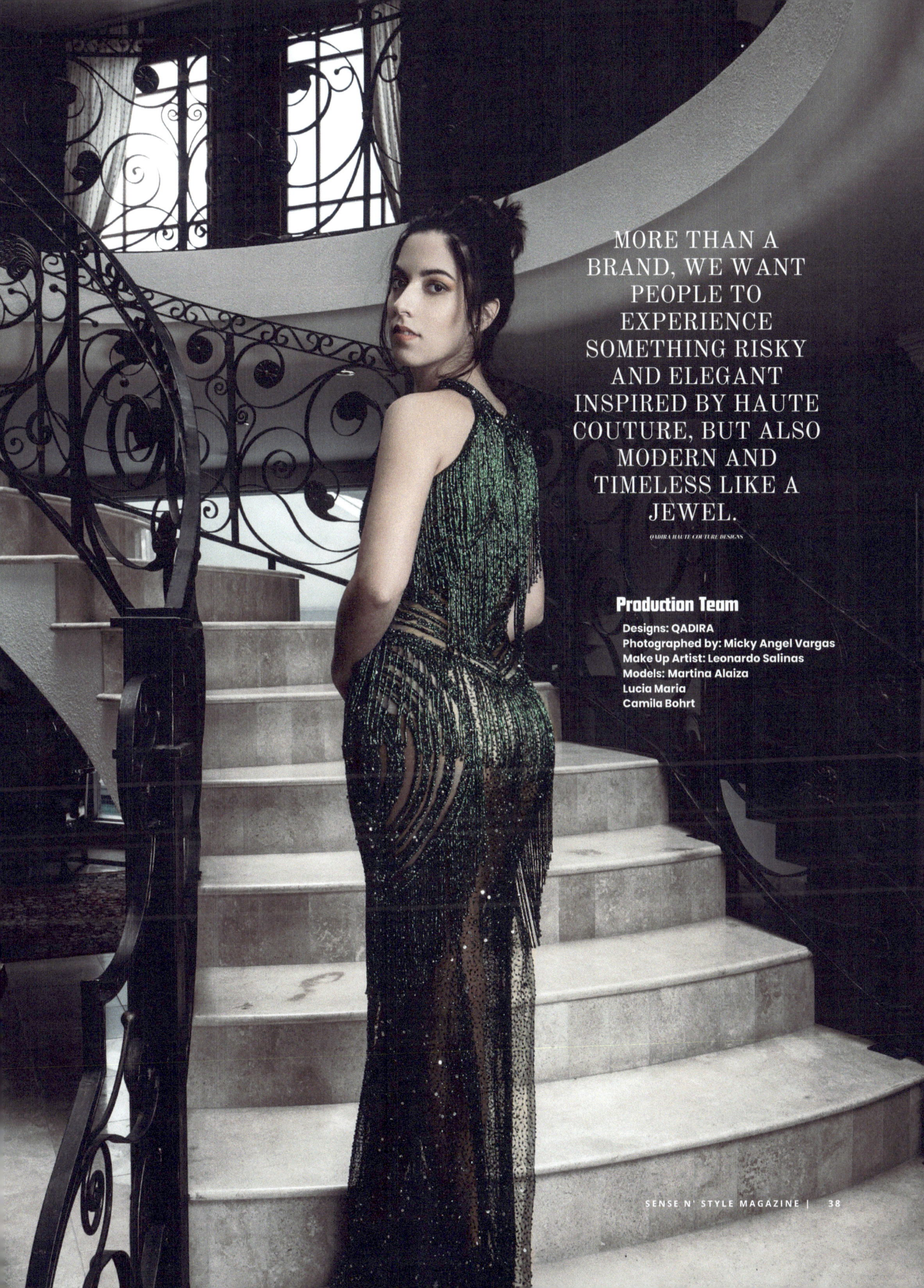

> MORE THAN A BRAND, WE WANT PEOPLE TO EXPERIENCE SOMETHING RISKY AND ELEGANT INSPIRED BY HAUTE COUTURE, BUT ALSO MODERN AND TIMELESS LIKE A JEWEL.
>
> *QADIRA HAUTE COUTURE DESIGNS*

Production Team

Designs: QADIRA
Photographed by: Micky Angel Vargas
Make Up Artist: Leonardo Salinas
Models: Martina Alaiza
Lucia Maria
Camila Bohrt

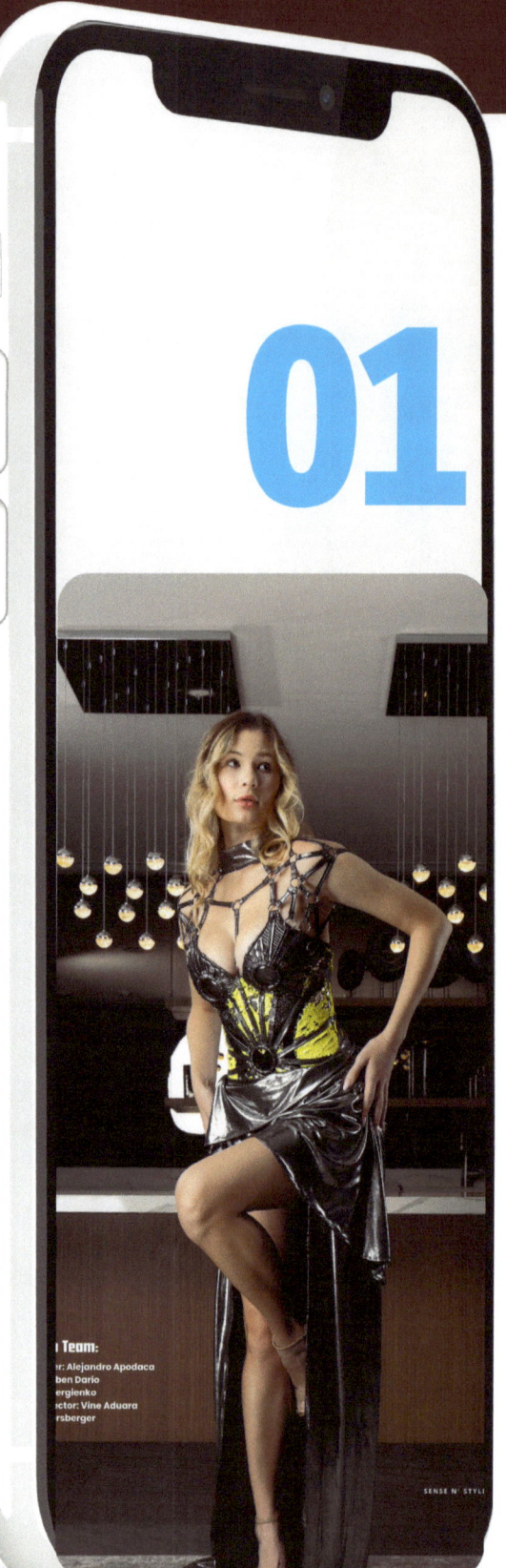

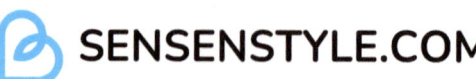 SENSENSTYLE.COM

SENSE N' STYLE APP

Designed specifically to help you stay connected and network within the fashion industry.

www.sensenstyle.com

SCAN TO BOOK A CONSULTATION

JOIN THE SENSE N' STYLE APP TODAY - BOOK A CONSULTATION TO GET STARTED!!!

We're thrilled to announce the upcoming launch of our new app, designed specifically to help you stay connected, network, and get more job opportunities within the fashion industry.

Whether you're a designer, model, photographer, or influencer, this app will be your go-to platform for discovering new opportunities, collaborating on projects, and staying up-to-date with the latest trends.

Don't miss out on being part of this amazing community! Join our waitlist today to be among the first to experience the app.

Subscribe to Sense N' Style Magazine to receive exclusive updates, insights, and tips directly from industry insiders. Stay connected, stay inspired, and take your fashion career to the next level!

SENSENSTYLE.COM

SENSE N' STYLE APP

Designed specifically to help you stay connected and network within the fashion industry.

www.sensenstyle.com

The best way to stay connected in the fashion industry!

01

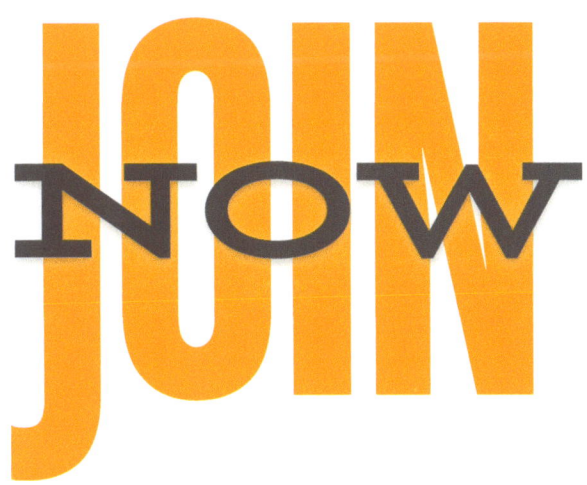

JOIN NOW

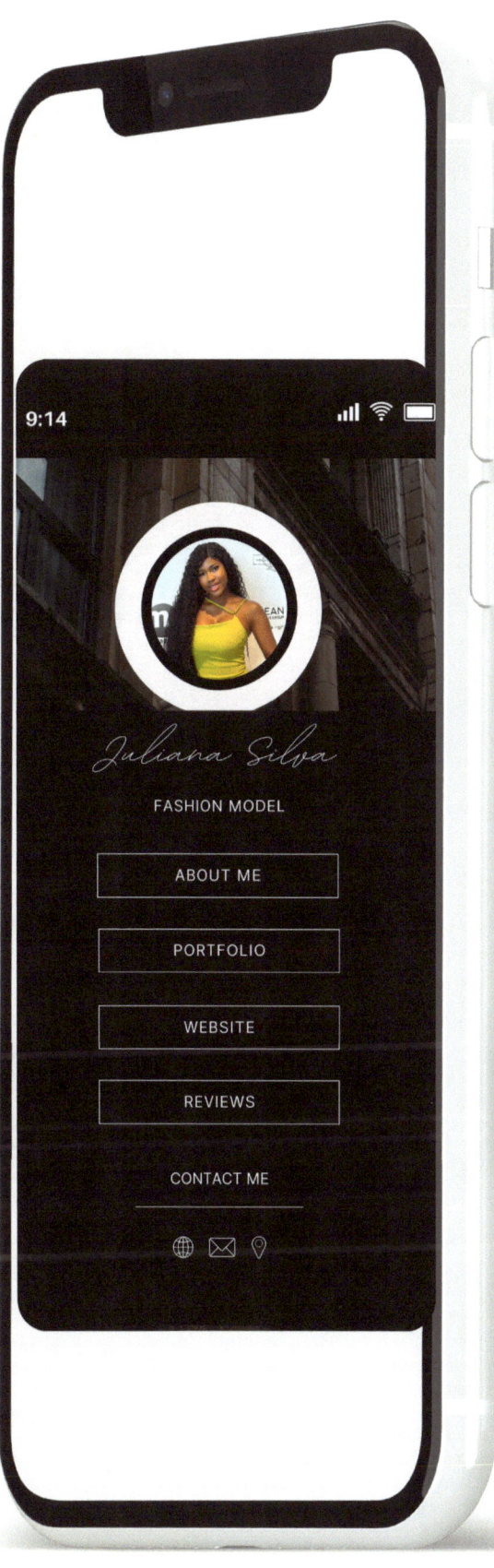

Subscribe to Sense N' Style Magazine to receive exclusive updates, insights, and tips directly from industry insiders. Stay connected, stay inspired, and take your fashion career to the next level!

THE INSIDER'S LOOK: YEAR-END MOMENTUM IN WOMEN'S EMPOWERMENT

As we move into the new year, the momentum of 2024 serves as a reminder that women are not only shaping the future but also redefining what empowerment looks like across industries.

A As the year wraps up, the intersection of fashion, politics, and business has showcased incredible momentum in women's empowerment, reflecting the diverse ways in which women are shaping industries and influencing global narratives.

In fashion, 2024 saw the rise of women led brands breaking traditional molds and prioritizing inclusivity and sustainability. From high fashion houses like Gabriela Hearst redefining luxury with eco conscious designs to streetwear brands amplifying female voices, the industry has become a platform for social change. Major fashion weeks featured collections that not only celebrated creativity but also carried messages of gender equity, with designers dedicating shows to women's rights movements and using their runways as stages for activism. Politics has also seen women leveraging style as a tool of empowerment. Female leaders around the globe have made deliberate choices that symbolize strength and identity, such as Kamala Harris's tailored suits or Sanna Marin's modern take on power dressing. These choices remind us that fashion is more than aesthetic; it's a medium for communication and cultural commentary. The increasing presence of women in political spaces also highlights their ability to influence policies that impact the fashion industry, such as those advocating for fair trade and ethical labor practices.

In the business world, women are pushing boundaries like never before. Leaders such as Stella McCartney have merged fashion with business acumen, championing sustainability and influencing corporate models worldwide. On the entrepreneurial front, women owned brands are thriving, thanks to innovative business models that prioritize community building and collaboration. Startups in fashion tech, for instance, are bridging the gap between style and functionality, empowering women to incorporate their professional and personal aesthetics effortlessly.

This year has also highlighted the importance of mentorship and networking in women's empowerment across these fields. Events like female driven fashion summits, political forums, and business expos have created spaces for collaboration and knowledge sharing, fostering a new generation of leaders. Such initiatives underscore the collective power of women united in their pursuits, whether they're walking the runway, leading a boardroom, or advocating for change in the political arena.

As we move into the new year, the momentum of 2024 serves as a reminder that women are not only shaping the future but also redefining what empowerment looks like across industries. The synergy between fashion, politics, and business is a testament to the multifaceted roles women continue to embrace, proving that empowerment isn't confined to one sphere, it's a movement spanning all facets of life.

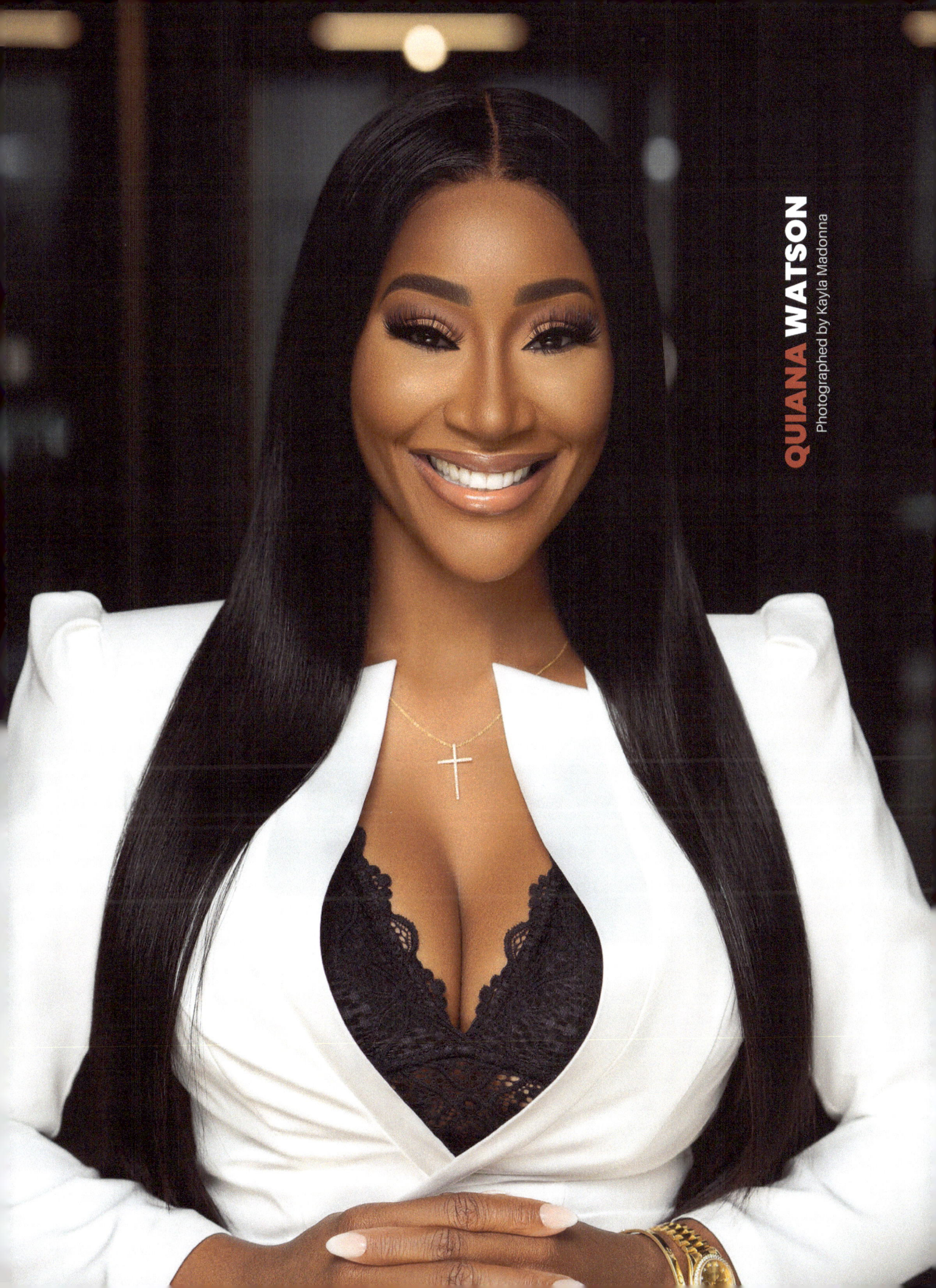

QUIANA WATSON

Photographed by Kayla Madonna

Dashboard
Sense N' Style Magazine

Sometimes it can be difficult to articulate the power of style and fashion through words, but with the help of a great team, we hope this edition was able to show how powerful the fashion industry is becoming.

We hope you enjoyed the read!

SENSENSTYLE.com
The New Fashion Experience

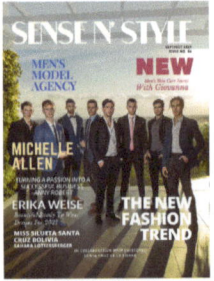
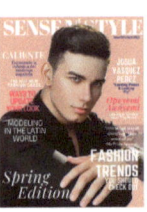
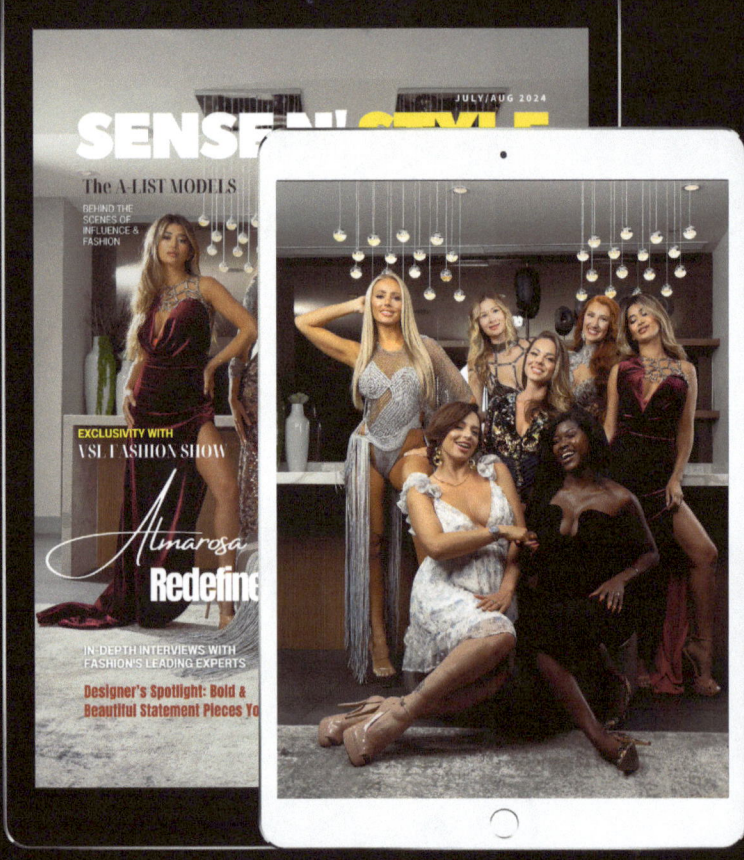
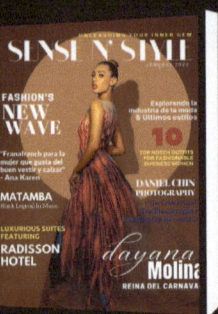
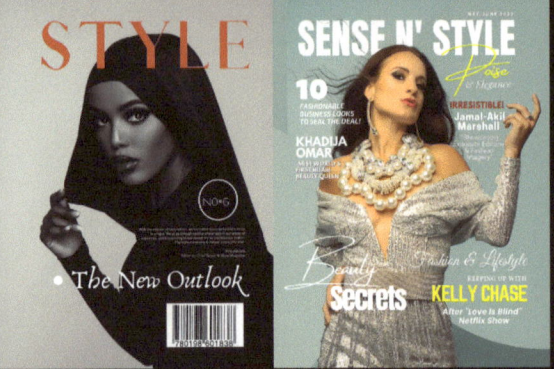
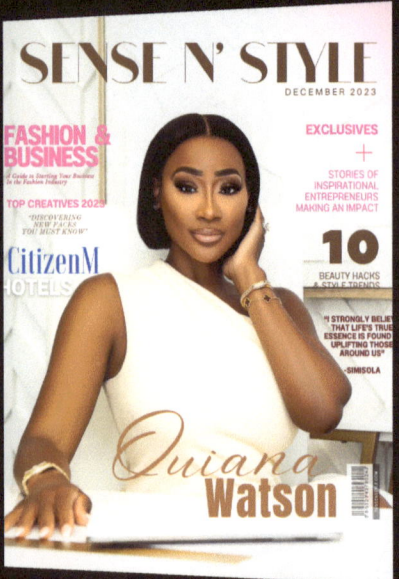

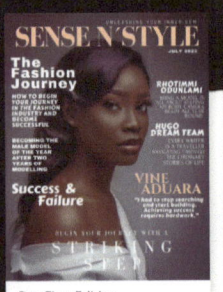

Our First Edition
The first edition of Sense N' Style was released in July 2020.

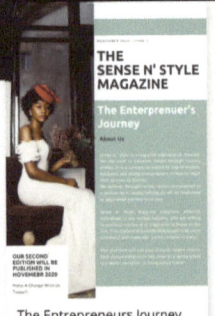

The Entrepreneurs Journey

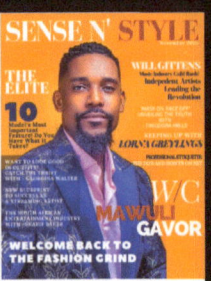

Our Second Edition
The second edition of Sense N' Style was officially released in November 2020.

Reach Out To Us

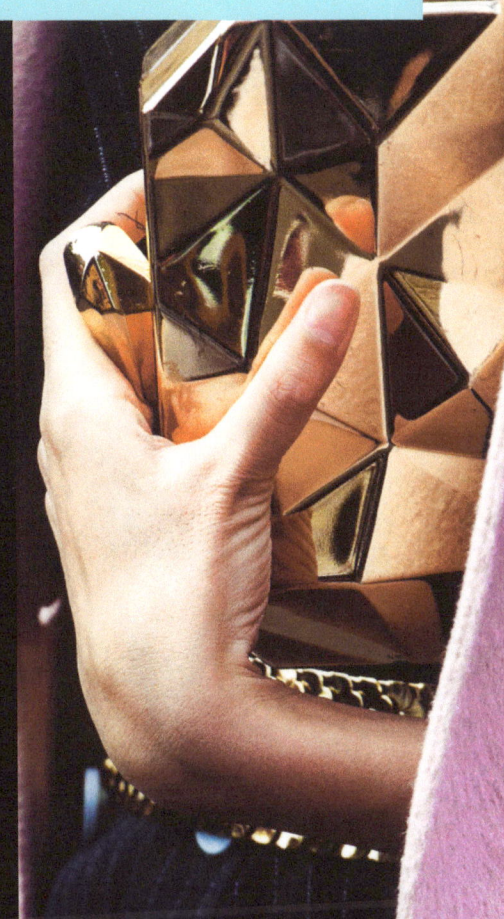

ABOUT US

Sense N' Style Magazine is a Fashion Magazine published in print & digital.

From the release of our first edition to date, we have worked with great minds to make our fashion magazine one of the best in the industry. With a team of experts boasting extensive experience in the field, our aim is to provide our readers with all the novelties of fashion easily accessible for them to learn current trends.

WHERE YOU CAN FIND US

WEBSITE

www.sensenstyle.com

STORES

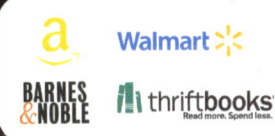

SOCIAL MEDIA

LinkedIn: Sense N' Style Magazine
Instagram: @sense_n_style_magazine
Twitter: @sensenstyle

KEEP IN TOUCH

(1) 857 210 4787 | (254) 743709849
info@sensenstyle.org
sierra@sensenstyle.org